THE GATE OF NUMBER

THE FOUR GATES TO THE HEAVENLIES:

An Invitation to Divine Collaboration Through the Voice of Christ on Angels

THE GATE OF NUMBER:

The plural was not just grammar. It was glory.

ANTONIN AZOTI

IMPACT WISDOM CREATIVE HOUSE

Cedar Rapids, IA, USA

The Gate of Number

We want to hear from you. Please send your comments about this book to us, in care of the address below. Thank you.

© 2025 Antonin Kodjo P. Azoti

All rights reserved.

No part of this publication may be reproduced, stored in a retrieval system, or transmitted in any form or by any means, electronic, mechanical, photocopying, recording, or otherwise, without the prior written permission of the author or publisher, except for brief quotations used in reviews, articles, or academic citation.

All Scripture quotations, unless otherwise noted, are taken from the Holy Bible, New International Version®, NIV®. Copyright © 1973, 1978, 1984, 2011 by Biblica, Inc.™ Used by permission. All rights reserved worldwide.

Scriptures marked KJV are from the King James Version. Public domain.

Cover design and interior formatting by Impact Wisdom Creative House. Cover represents an army of a multitude of humans and Heavenly Host standing ready for combat.1

First Edition

Printed in Cedar Rapids, IA, USA 52404

ISBN: 978-1-969612-00-8

For permissions, inquiries, or bulk orders, contact:

iw.creativehouse@gmail.com

www.thefourgatestotheheavenlies.org

This publication is intended for spiritual enrichment and theological reflection. The insights presented reflect the author's personal study, convictions, and journey of faith. They are not intended to replace the authority of Scripture, the guidance of the Holy Spirit, or wise spiritual counsel.

Published by Impact Wisdom Creative House, Cedar Rapids, IA, USA

This book may not be used for commercial purposes without express written permission. All rights reserved under international copyright conventions and protections.

VI

To The Seal Breakers

"He telleth the number of the stars; he calleth them all by their names." (Psalm 147:4)

The Gate of Number

Acknowledgements

All thanks be to God, Father, Son, and Holy Spirit, the Initiator of this journey and the ever-present Helper. This book would not exist without His prompting, His patience, and His partnership.

And to the Heavenly Hosts themselves, this book is, in many ways, about you. I do not thank you as we thank men, but I honor the mystery of your nearness. There were moments in this journey when I felt your presence, like silent companions watching and waiting, even at times pleading gently and earnestly for me to return to the writing. I could sense your alignment with Heaven's desire for this message to come forth. Your holy urging was a kind of intercession I will not forget.

To the voices of Christian ministries whose messages, teachings, and lifestyles helped break the seals of this generation, thank you. Apostles, prophets, evangelists, pastors, and teachers, some known by name, others known by impact, your faithfulness opened hearts and stirred longing for divine collaboration. You watered seeds I didn't yet know were planted.

To the staff and partners of Winds International, thank you for walking this kingdom vision with me. You are chosen. Your commitment to prayer, your endurance through challenges, and your shared burden for global impact made this writing not only possible, but deeply meaningful. I am honored to serve alongside you.

To Wycliffe Africa, and its Director, Mr. Edwyn Kiptness, thank you for creating an environment where spiritual growth, vision, and belonging are nurtured. You made it a place one can always look back to as home. Your leadership continues to inspire.

To the churches that helped shape my walk with the Lord: Hus Presbyterian Church, Grace Street Church, Hope Lutheran Church, River of Life Church and Église Baptiste Internationale – Centre d'Adoration (EBICA)

Each one contributed threads of strength, insight, and communion that helped weave the spiritual fabric of this book.

To the Hope Lutheran Men's Fellowship, thank you. You were more than brothers in Christ; you were a crew of strong, loving men who lent not just moral support, but practical and financial help along the way. Your encouragement carried weight.

To my work families in Cedar Rapids, Iowa, thank you for being more than educators and professionals. You created uplifting spaces where writing could breathe. I'm honored to be part of schools that carry not just academic excellence, but human warmth and encouragement. Your quiet support helped make this book possible, and I hope it makes you proud.

And to the Fourth Grade Class of 2024–2025 at Hiawatha, thank you for being little angels in disguise. Week after week, your curiosity, your cheers, and your persistent questions about "the book" gave me joy. Some of you asked to be named in it, know that you're forever part of the story.

To the families and friends who were more than blood or acquaintances and some of whom agreed to read and give us their impressions on the first drafts of this work: Ablode, Agbetowofana, Porter, Westerhoft, Madjedje, Apedey, Troendle, Schehl, Huttar and Jawitz. Thank you for your generosity, prayers, and presence. You each brought encouragement in ways that mattered most.

To my extended family, especially my younger brother Silver Mahirezewa, thank you for standing by me through financial and moral support, and for opening doors that helped me keep moving.

And finally, to my beloved family, Sarah, Jerome, Giovanni, Victoria, and Ebenezer, this book came at the cost

The Gate of Number

of long hours and quiet sacrifices. You gave me the space to listen, think, and write. You paid a price I will never forget. Thank you for walking with me.

This book was written with Heaven's help, but also with yours.

* * *

Disclaimer

The individuals, churches, institutions, and organizations mentioned in this Acknowledgments section are recognized for their impact, support, and presence in my journey. Their inclusion does not imply endorsement of the theological positions, interpretations, or conclusions presented in this book. The responsibility for all content, perspectives, and interpretations rests solely with the author.

PREFACE

This book began as a footnote.

I was writing on the Great Commission when something unexpected caught my attention: the consistent presence of the Heavenly Hosts, Angels, in the events stretching from the resurrection of Jesus to the proclamation of the Commission itself. It was not merely symbolic. It was not incidental. It seemed deliberate.

Could it be that these heavenly beings were not just observers of the mission, but intended participants? Could it be that the Great Commission was never meant to be fulfilled by the earthly family of God alone, but in unity with His heavenly one?

I could not ignore these questions. I intended only to pause briefly, to make a small note on what Jesus said about Angels. But that pause became a path. The footnote became a journey. And this volume is its first unfolding.

A Journey of Awakening

My own journey with the invisible realm began long before I could explain it. I was raised in a home that believed in the existence of a supreme being, an unseen presence capable of providing, protecting, and answering prayer.

The Gate of Number

XIV

Though this being was first introduced to me in a traditional form, through the clay figure named *Atta* to whom my grandmother offered sacrifices, the sense of an invisible sovereign was planted deep in my soul.

At six years old, I became Catholic. By thirteen, I had completed all the rites of the Church and developed a deep admiration for the lives of the Saints. I loved reading about their devotion, their visions, their witness. That spiritual hunger carried into my young adulthood. At nineteen, after hearing a Gospel presentation, I prayed the sinner's prayer and joined a Baptist church. For the next six years, I immersed myself in Scripture, attended every church meeting I could, served in multiple ministries, and poured myself into missions.

During that season, I also began to perceive the presence of Angels. Sometimes it was through vision, like the two majestic figures I once saw standing guard at the church entrance, swords drawn. Other times it was simply a knowing: a human figure encountered, whose ordinariness could not hide a supernatural presence. I cannot explain how I knew. But I knew.

Though these experiences never ceased, the absence of teaching left me with little clarity on how to understand or develop them. My Baptist community, while sincere and warm, offered no framework for Angelic ministry. My visions were received with silence. And over time, though I remained grateful for the interventions I sensed, I did not know how to respond further. The encounters continued. But I grew distant from them.

A Growing Burden

More than a decade ago, I transitioned from remote mission fields to life in a city, and with that came greater access to teaching from beyond my geography. I began to hear testimonies, some incredible, about Angelic interaction. Some stories stirred my spirit; others felt difficult to accept. Yet my desire to understand deepened.

Still, I was cautious. My roots in traditional evangelical theology kept me from embracing anything that lacked scriptural grounding. I longed for systematic teaching from those who had these experiences, teaching that could demonstrate scriptural faithfulness. I could not pursue those encounters firsthand. But I could return to the Word. And so I did.

As I continued searching the Scriptures, studying books and articles, particularly those dealing with the Great Commission, I found myself drawn into questions I had not anticipated. Why was the Church, with all its resources, making such slow progress in completing the mission Christ gave us? Why, with so many organizations and so much blessing, do we see so little coordinated breakthrough in the hardest fields?

I began to wonder: Are we missing something? Are we truly using all the resources Heaven has made available?

An Unexpected Discovery

What surprised me most in this journey was that Jesus, though He offered no systematic teaching on Angels, said enough to unveil powerful truths. Once I stopped and pondered His words, I found that His brief references carried layers of design, strategy, and invitation. What He did not say in quantity, He made up for in precision. His grammar, His timing, even His silences, carried weight.

This series is born out of that realization.

Though I was originally writing on the Great Commission, I stumbled upon a pattern that reshaped my focus: the involvement of Angels was not occasional, it was integral. That led to new questions. What is their role today? How do we relate to them as fellow servants? What responsibility do we bear in the collaboration God intended between His earthly and heavenly family?

In pursuing these questions, I came to a sobering insight: we may be attempting to fulfill a divine assignment with only part of the intended workforce. Without unity between the

Church on earth and the Hosts of Heaven, we may be laboring with incomplete strength.

This book is a contribution to correcting that gap.

The Human Connection

Yet the most transformative revelation I received through this journey was not about Angels directly, it was about us.

The more I studied, the more I saw that the path into deep, meaningful collaboration with Angels runs through a very human gate: the heart. The heart that is aligned with theirs. The heart that serves. The heart that reflects Heaven's way of seeing and treating others.

The more we cultivate the right posture toward fellow humans, the more we open ourselves to the atmosphere in which Angels dwell. After all, Scripture says some have entertained Angels unaware, not in heavenly visions, but in ordinary hospitality (Hebrews 13:2). Perhaps we've rejected Angels because we have rejected one another. And perhaps the key to accessing Angelic support lies not just in prayer or theology, but in how we treat each other.

This was not an easy insight to accept. But the more I sought God for understanding, the more it settled in me. The book you hold in your hands emerged from that search.

The Gate of Number

XVIII

A Final Word

Near the end of writing this first volume, I was led to read a few recent Christian writings on the Church.

I am deeply humbled by the clarity, research, and pastoral insight that mark many of them. I realized a widespread concern for the spiritual health and missional vitality of the Church. I align with those. The words of those writers stirred a renewed sense of urgency in me, not only for what we must do, but how we must become.

We live in a generation suffering a crisis of behavior, of identity, of direction. In such a time, the Church must rediscover its unity, not just among its members on earth, but in fellowship with Heaven. The Angels who long to serve with us are waiting for us to resemble them in how we serve each other.

This book is an invitation into that journey.

It does not claim final answers. It offers discoveries, mine, and perhaps soon, yours. I pray you will add your own footnotes to the ongoing revelation of Heaven's intention. May your questions deepen. May your heart open. And may we, together, move toward the fullness of the fulfillment of the Commission Christ entrusted to both families, earthly and heavenly, for the sake of His Kingdom on earth.

The Author

TABLE OF CONTENTS

ACKNOWLEDGEMENTS	IX
PREFACE	XIII
A Journey of Awakening	XIII
A Growing Burden	XV
An Unexpected Discovery	XVI
The Human Connection	XVII
A Final Word	XVIII
TABLE OF CONTENTS	1
GENERAL INTRODUCTION TO THE SERIES:	
THE FOUR GATES TO THE HEAVENLIES	7
Not a Systematic Angelology	9
Why This Matters	10
The Four Gates	11
A Mission for This Generation	12
A Word to the Reader	13
On Language and Terminology	13
INTRODUCTION TO THE FIRST GATE: THE GATE OF NUMBER	
	15
LIGHT ON THE NUMBER	22
Why Focus on a Plural?	23
How We'll Explore This Gate	24

The Gate of Number

LANGUAGE: A VESSEL FOR THE INVISIBLE	24
LANGUAGE SHIFTS MIRROR SPIRITUAL SHIFTS	25
WHY RED LETTERS MATTER	27
WHY PLURAL FORM MATTERS SPIRITUALLY	28
STARS: WHERE NUMBER MEETS THE SPIRITUAL	29
THE FOUR DIMENSIONS OF THE NUMBER GATE	30

CHAPTER 1

THE NUMBER OF REVERENCE.   35

WHEN PLURAL MEANS GLORY	35
FROM HEBREW ROOTS TO GLOBAL REACH	37
WHEN LANGUAGE BOWS: THE HEBREW GRAMMAR OF MAJESTY	39
REVERENCE ACROSS TONGUES: WHAT TRANSLATION CAN'T HIDE	43
HEAVEN'S TONE: HOW JESUS REVEALED THE REVERENCE OF GOD	46
REVERENCE IS THE ATMOSPHERE OF HEAVEN	50
REVERENT EYES: THE FIRST GATE INTO THE HEAVENLY WORLD	54

CHAPTER 2

COLLECTIVE REPRESENTATION   60

WHEN SILENCE SPEAKS	60
THE HEAVENLY LOGIC OF COLLECTIVE IDENTITY	63
HOW PLURAL LANGUAGE REVEALS KINGDOM ALIGNMENT	66
THE TRINITY: HEAVEN'S FIRST COMMUNITY	66
REPRESENTATION AS THE RHYTHM OF HEAVEN AND EARTH	66
WE BELONG TO THE FAMILY OF HEAVEN	68

CHAPTER 3

THE NUMBER OF A MULTITUDE   74

A Word That Holds a World	74
The Sagan number	76
Scripture's Witness to Angelic Multitudes	78
Patmos and the Assembly Beyond Number	80
The Assurance of the Multitude	84
Elisha and the Eyes of Faith	86
The Great Multitude and the Eternal Family	89
Surrounded by Thousands	92

CHAPTER 4

SINGULAR MULTIPLEXITY — 98

Understanding Multiplexity	98
Angels: a diverse types of pluralities	101
Heavenly Hosts and Heavenly Realms	107
Beyond what humans can know	109
Multiplexity is part of the Universe	112
The God who knows complexities	115
Embracing the Complexity of Divine Design	118

PART II.

THE PATH TO THE NUMBER — 124

Walking the Earth in Step with Heaven	124
Walking into the Practice of Heavenly Partnership	125
Jesus and the Angelic Life	126
Angels Still Walk Among Us	128
The Hosts Still Move. The Church Must Respond.	129
A Call to Discernment and Accountability	130
The Principle Beneath the Path	130

From Mystery to Walking	132
A Word to the Individual Heart	133
The Hidden Link: Angels and How We Treat Each Other	134
What's Ahead	134

CHAPTER 5

REVERENCE: THE POSTURE OF DESTINY — 138

Introduction	138
Divine Help and Provision Are Available	139
Reverence Is a Gate	141
The Environment of the Host	142
Irreverence and the Grieving of the Host	143
Jesus, the Model of Reverence	144
Walking It Out in Every Sphere of Life	144
Final Invitation: Reverence as a Way of Life	151

CHAPTER 6

UNITY: THE POSTURE OF PARTNERSHIP WITH HEAVEN — 155

Introduction	155
A Reflection of Trinity	157
Unique Principles of Heavenly Unity	159
When Church Walls Came Down	168
Unity Attitudes, Values, and Behaviors	171
We Are Not Isolate Champions	176

CHAPTER 7

ASSURANCE: BEING A PART OF THOUSANDS — 181

| Living in the Assurance of Angelic Presence | 181 |

THE SPIRITUAL REALITY OF BEING PART OF GOD'S IMMENSE HOUSEHOLD — 182

FROM THEOLOGY TO APPLICATION: WELCOMING THE UNSEEN SUPPORT INTO EVERY DOMAIN OF LIFE — 185

- ACCESSING THE ANGELIC SUPPORT ASSIGNED TO YOUR DESTINY — 195
- THE PATHWAY OF FAITH. — 196
- ENJOYING THE POWER OF 'THE MULTITUDE'. — 198
- LIVING ASSURANCE IN ACTION — 210
- DEPLOYING THE MULTITUDE. — 222
- INTEGRATING THE REVELATION OF THE MULTITUDE IN YOUR PRAYER LIFE. — 226

CHAPTER 8

HUMILITY: THE CALL OF THE INCOMPREHENSIBLE — 237

WALKING IN COLLABORATION WITH THE ANGELIC HOSTS: HUMILITY IN ACTION — 237

- THE CHARACTER OF CONNECTION — 251
- CONDUCTS TO GROW AS WE WALK THE PATH — 259
- THE POSTURE THAT UNLOCKS THE UNSEEN — 276

CONCLUSION TO THE FIRST GATE: THE GATE OF NUMBER — 280

EPILOGUE — I

APPENDIX — III

- GLOSSARY OF KEY TERMS — III
- COMMUNITY & MOVEMENT — XVIII
- EXPLORE THE JOURNEY FURTHER — XIX

The Gate of Number

6

ABOUT THE AUTHOR   XXI

General Introduction to the Series:

The Four Gates to the Heavenlies

What if one of the most underutilized resources in the fulfillment of the Great Commission is not on earth, but in Heaven? What if, embedded within the words of Jesus, are keys that open access to a realm of divine collaboration we have long overlooked?

The subject of Angels often evokes mixed reactions. Some approach the idea with faith and reverence. Others meet it with suspicion, hesitation, or quiet confusion. In many circles, Angels are discussed with poetic nostalgia or dismissed as literary symbols. And it is true: the concept of Angels has not enjoyed universal consensus, either in religious traditions or in modern theological thought.

Across mythological, mystical, and religious literature, numerous spiritual or disembodied beings are described. But the Angelic order as understood in monotheistic religion, and especially in Christianity, is distinct. Even here, however, interpretation is far from monolithic. Some believers affirm Angels as literal beings, ministers of God with personality, will, and assigned function. Others, influenced by modern rationalism or liberal theology, interpret them as symbolic personifications, ethical illustrations of God's protective care, or metaphors of divine presence.

This variety of interpretation is not new. Theologians such as Louis Berkhof have outlined a wide range of historical positions: from Roman Catholics who affirm Angels as pure spirits, to early Protestants who attributed to them a form of spiritual corporeality; from Swedenborg's belief that all Angels were once humans, to Rationalist denials of their existence altogether. Still, Berkhof concludes with clarity: *"No one who bows before the authority of the Word of God can doubt the existence of Angels."*

> ***To bow to Scripture is to believe in Angels.***

That is the position from which this series is written.

For me, and for many believers who have encountered the reality of Angelic presence, the Hosts of Heaven are neither abstractions nor literary devices. They are real. They are relational. They are part of the household of God. And though their substance may differ from the matter we are accustomed to, their presence and participation in the divine economy are consistent, coherent, and compelling.

This series does not seek to settle all doctrinal debates. Nor does it dismiss the diversity of interpretive traditions.

General Introduction to the Series

Rather, it acknowledges that what may appear straightforward to some can seem unfamiliar or even unsettling to others. I write, therefore, with humility, but also with conviction. I do not speak from speculation. I speak from reverence for the Word of God and deep inquiry into the words of Jesus Himself.

Not a Systematic Angelology

Let me be clear: this series is not intended to serve as a comprehensive or systematic teaching on Angelology. There are already excellent theological works that serve that purpose, some of which I deeply respect and may build on in other writings. This series is something else. It is a focused invitation to rediscover what Jesus revealed about Angels through His own speech, not in volume, but in weight. It is a meditative, revelatory exploration of the gates that open when we pay close attention to His language.

The Gospels record relatively few direct statements from Jesus about Angels. But those statements, if observed with spiritual attentiveness, carry tremendous theological implications. They reflect not only Heaven's reality but Heaven's intent. And when studied together, they unveil a design: a divine architecture in which the Hosts of Heaven

> **What Jesus said about Angels may be few in words, but vast in weight.**

The Gate of Number

are not peripheral figures, but active collaborators in God's purpose for the world.

Why This Matters

The spiritual state of many believers today reflects a tragic disconnect from the fullness of God's provision. While the Church has grown in resources, structures, and strategies, it often struggles to walk in the power, unity, and clarity promised by the gospel. Too many are discouraged by a lack of spiritual breakthrough, disappointed in the transformation they had hoped to experience, or dulled by traditions that limit their vision of what is possible.

Yet, the provision of Heaven is still available.

Part of that provision is found in the Angelic realm. And yet we seldom access it. Not because it is beyond us, but because we have not been taught how to recognize it, honor it, or collaborate with it.

Heaven has not closed. Its provision still flows.

This series suggests that Jesus not only acknowledged the Heavenly Hosts, He included them in His vision for the Church. That is why this journey matters. It is not a detour from the Great Commission; it is a rediscovery of how

Heaven intended that Commission to be fulfilled in the first place: through alignment between the earthly and the heavenly family of God.

The Four Gates

This book is the first in a series titled *The Four Gates to the Heavenlies*. Each volume in the series reflects one of four dimensions revealed in Jesus' speech concerning Angels. These gates are:

1. **The Gate of Number** – unveiling the intentional use of the plural "Angels" in Christ's speech to reveal plurality, diversity, structure, and complexity within the Host.

2. **The Gate of Identity** – exploring what Jesus reveals about the nature, attributes, and distinct existence of Angels as beings who serve in unique relationship to the Father.

3. **The Gate of Reference** – examining the different phrases Jesus used when referring to Angels ("His Angels," "the Angels of God," etc.) and what each reveals about divine hierarchy, relational proximity, and mission.

4. **The Gate of Function** – revealing the roles assigned to Angels in Jesus' parables and teachings,

and what they tell us about their participation in judgment, gathering, protecting, and proclaiming.

Each gate represents a dimension of Heaven's design, a design meant not only to be understood, but to be walked in.

A Mission for This Generation

This series is not just a reflection. It is a mission. It calls the redeemed of this generation to go beyond the flattened models of a three-dimensional worldview and enter the spiritual space God intended His New Creation to operate from. It is time to shift from earth-bound paradigms into Heaven-led patterns. It is time to move beyond admiration of heavenly realities into alignment with them.

We do not explore the words of Jesus about Angels merely to expand our knowledge, but to uncover a lost partnership, a divine collaboration. The Host of Heaven is not a passive gallery of observers. They are participants in the unfolding plan of God, designed to work in harmony with the Church. As the writer of Hebrews reminds us, they are *"ministering spirits sent to serve those who will inherit salvation"* (Hebrews 1:14).

The Host of Heaven is not watching. They are working.

General Introduction to the Series

If the Great Commission is to be completed, it must be completed through the unity of the divine family, heavenly and earthly, Angelic and human, under the lordship of Christ. That unity is not automatic. It must be discerned. It must be cultivated. It must be walked in.

A Word to the Reader

This introduction is just the beginning. Some readers will come from traditions where these insights feel familiar. Others will find them new or even unsettling. That is expected. What I ask is not agreement, but openness. I write as a steward of what I have seen, not as a master of all that is. The journey continues, for me, and I pray, for you.

A second part of this introduction, *A General Introduction to the Series (Part 2)*, will offer more detail about the interpretive approach, theological framework, and hermeneutic commitments that guide this work.

On Language and Terminology

For clarity and simplicity, I will use the terms "Angel(s)" and "Heavenly Host(s)" interchangeably, although I recognize their theological distinctions. I follow the New Testament's precedent, and Jesus' usage, in preferring "Angels" as a default reference. Additionally, I will use the pronoun **"he"** as a generic form when referring to invisible beings, not out of insensitivity, but for linguistic economy. I trust readers will understand the intent.

INTRODUCTION TO THE FIRST GATE: THE GATE OF NUMBER

Not all truths are loud. Some rest in the quiet precision of a word.

When Jesus spoke of Angels, He did not spend chapters unfolding their theology. He gave us something more potent: a pattern of reference. And what strikes the attentive reader is not only what He said, but how He said it. Time and again, He chose the plural. "The Angels." Not an Angel. Not the Angel. The Angels.

> *He did not say "an Angel." He said "the Angels." And that changes everything.*

This book begins there.

The Gate of Number is the first of *The Four Gates to the Heavenlies*. It is not named for arithmetic, but for revelation. The consistent pluralization used by Jesus when referring to Angels is not grammatical convenience, it is theological intention. In that plural, a realm opens. It reveals that the Angelic reality is not singular, occasional, or symbolic. It is multiplied, structured, and intended for divine collaboration.

To those who have long considered Angels as rare visitors, appearing briefly in dreams, visions, or songs, the idea of their multitude may seem abstract. But Heaven does not function in isolated acts. It functions in orchestration. Scripture speaks of innumerable hosts (Hebrews 12:22), of legions (Matthew 26:53), of companies in ranks (Luke 2:13). Jesus' words confirm this. He speaks not of a lone agent, but of a coordinated multitude. And He does so as the One who knows them intimately, not only as Creator, but as Commander.

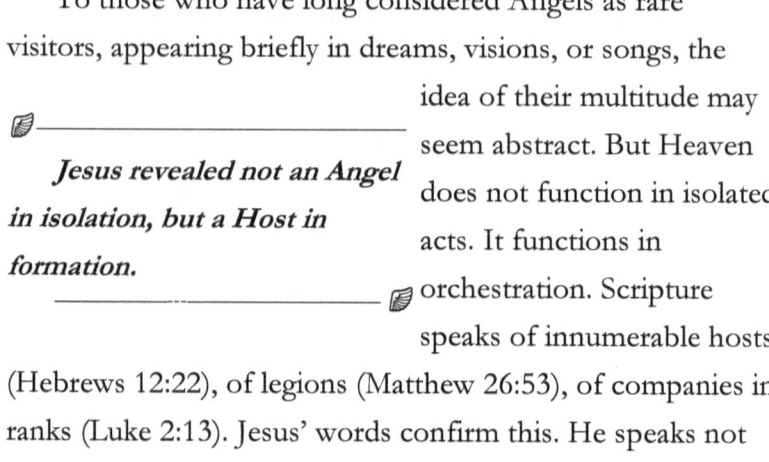

Jesus revealed not an Angel in isolation, but a Host in formation.

This Gate invites us to take seriously what this plurality reveals: that the Hosts of Heaven are diverse, ranked, aligned, and present. They are not metaphors to admire from afar. They are family, spiritual brothers in service to the same Father, partners under the same Commission. The use of the plural is a subtle yet powerful unveiling of how God works, not only through His Spirit and His Word, but through His many messengers, assigned in wisdom, dispatched in unity, and waiting for partnership.

Yet most believers have not been taught to think this way.

The idea of Angels, let alone their diversity and collaboration, has too often been reduced to poetic allusion

Light on the Number

or mystical excess. In many theological circles, they are marginalized, abstracted, or spiritualized into symbols. But Jesus did not speak in symbols alone. He spoke in truth. And His consistent use of the plural must arrest us. It must lead us to ask: What is He revealing by this? And what are we missing when we ignore it?

This Gate is a threshold. When we cross it, we begin to see Heaven not as a single throne in the sky, but as a realm of living order, a divine community whose members are not spectators, but servants, messengers, protectors, and agents of the will of God. We begin to see that God's heavenly family is as real, as organized, and as purposeful as His earthly one, and that both are meant to work together.

More than that, this Gate sets the foundation for the journey ahead. If we cannot perceive the plurality of the Hosts, we will never discern their identity, their function, or the precision of the ways in which Jesus referred to them. Each of those awaits us in the next Gates. But this first Gate opens the others.

In the chapters that follow, we will walk slowly. We will examine Jesus' use of the plural. We will look at the moments He chose to refer to Angels, not just what He said, but what He implied. We will consider the spiritual implications of number: not just how many there are, but why that multiplicity matters. Why it reflects a design. Why it opens the possibility for collaboration between realms.

The Gate of Number

You do not need to be a scholar to enter this Gate. You need only hunger for clarity. What Jesus revealed in His grammar is meant to be seen. And once seen, it changes everything, not just how we understand Angels, but how we understand our own place in God's Kingdom.

Let us walk through the Gate of Number. Heaven is not singular. And neither is our mission.

This book is divided into two parts, each one carrying a distinct but connected purpose.

Part 1 is a revelatory exposition. It opens the Gate of Number by examining Jesus' repeated use of the plural term "Angels." What emerges from that simple grammatical detail is a layered unveiling of Heaven's design. This first section brings forward four key revelations:

> *In a plural word, Heaven's pattern unfolds.*

- Reverence – Heaven's order is built on the fear of the Lord.

- Collective Representation – The Hosts serve as one, revealing the relational unity of Heaven.

- Multitude – The Angelic realm is vast, intentional, and ready.

Light on the Number

- Complexity – God's design is layered, multi-dimensional, and orchestrated.

- These are not theological curiosities. They are invitations to posture.

That is why Part 2 of the book shifts from revelation to activation. It translates the truths uncovered into walkable steps, four postures that align us with Heaven's way:

- Reverence – that restores awe and alignment with God's holiness.

- Unity – that mirrors Heaven's harmony and invites divine partnership.

- Assurance – that rests in God's strategic governance and provision.

- Humility – that opens the heart to mystery, complexity, and surrendered obedience.

This journey is not merely intellectual. It is relational. It invites your heart, your habits, and your community into transformation.

To help guide that process, each major section concludes with questions for reflection. These are designed for personal meditation or group discussion. You may want to pause, journal, pray, or share. The content is meant to be absorbed slowly. Don't rush. Let the Spirit speak.

Finally, remember: the purpose of this book is not to produce a theory of Angels. It is to open a gate, so that you may walk through it into a deeper collaboration with Heaven. If you engage it with openness, reverence, and readiness, that gate will not only open. It will invite you to stay.

Part I

Light on the Number

There is a gate in Jesus' words, quiet, deliberate, and easily overlooked, hidden not in what He declared, but *how* He said it. At first glance, this may seem like a grammatical footnote, a subtle linguistic habit.

Sometimes the deepest gates are not declared-they are whispered.

But as we begin to study the words of Jesus closely, we find that this is no accident. It is this seemingly small yet spiritually charged grammatical choice that this volume explores. The insights shared here are the fruit of years of prayerful reflection and study, drawn from deep meditation on every passage in which Jesus speaks of angels. What becomes clear is that not once does He use the singular. Every time, He says *"angels."* This is the Gate of Number. It opens with the Lord's exclusive use of the plural form when referring to angels.

I've studied, wrestled, and sought the Lord over these verses. I do not claim that every layer has been uncovered. Yet I believe that the clarity, strength, and spiritual resonance of Jesus' language make this journey through the Gate of Number both valuable and necessary for the Church today.

When the Son speaks with precision, the Church must listen with reverence.

That kind of consistency in the mouth of the Son of God invites our attention.

Why Focus on a Plural?

At this point, you may rightly ask: Why focus so intensely on one linguistic detail? Can something as technical as "plural form" really carry deep spiritual meaning? These are fair questions. Important ones. And perhaps, for some, the answer is already obvious. You may be one of those who has learned, either through study or experience, that the Spirit of God often hides revelation in the details, even in grammar, symbolism, and speech patterns. You've seen before how what seems insignificant becomes a door to greater understanding.

But for others, your starting place might be curiosity, or even doubt. You might be wondering, "Am I really supposed to build spiritual insight on something as subtle as this?"

That is why I want to walk slowly at first. These opening pages are not just theological scaffolding, they are a bridge. They will help you understand the context and prepare your heart for the insight that follows. Even if this initial reasoning doesn't fully persuade you, I encourage you to keep reading. Often, the Spirit of truth confirms in our hearts what the mind only begins to understand. The clarity will come. And when it does, I believe it will not be mere information, but revelation.

How We'll Explore This Gate

To help you walk through this gate, we'll begin by looking at the nature and power of language itself. We'll consider how speech, structure, and silence work in tandem to express reality, both human and divine. From there, we'll zoom in on the category of grammatical number, specifically the plural, and how that functions in the biblical languages Jesus used or referenced. Then, step by step, we'll unpack how Jesus' deliberate use of the plural form when speaking of angels was not just stylistic, but spiritually strategic.

This first part of the book lays the theological and spiritual foundation. Part II will help us walk out the implications in real life.

Language: A Vessel for the Invisible

Let's begin with the basics. Language is not just words. It includes silence, gesture, rhythm, tone, breath, and space. It's the atmosphere in which thought takes form. Every person speaks with layers of meaning, some intentional, some unconscious. The same is true in Scripture. The Holy Spirit inspired not only the messages, but the method.

Light on the Number

When Jesus spoke, He wasn't simply delivering doctrine, He was revealing the texture of Heaven. His words formed a kind of spiritual landscape. His language choices weren't casual; they were full of weight, depth, and purpose.

The red letters do not just inform. They direct.

This is why we must pay attention to what He said, and how He said it. Because changes in language usage made a difference in history, we can expect today that a change whether suggested or initiated unintentionally, there is subtle call to change. The next two sections will illustrate that more.

Language Shifts Mirror Spiritual Shifts

Throughout history, changes in language have often accompanied deeper transformations, shifts in culture, spirituality, and civilization.

Take the Great Vowel Shift in English, a major phonetic transformation between the 15th and 17th centuries. At first glance, it may seem like a purely academic event. But this linguistic transition mirrored sweeping historical forces: the aftermath of the Black Death, the rise of humanism, the invention of the printing press, the Reformation, and the dawn of the Renaissance.

Language was not evolving in isolation. It was shifting because the world was shifting. New ideas, new spiritual hunger, and new ways of seeing the world needed new words and sounds to express them.

And crucially, out of that era came the King James Bible, a translation that would give shape to the spiritual vocabulary of millions.

The Name "Angel" and the Power of Usage

Let's now consider the word itself: "angel". It comes from the Hebrew *malak*, meaning *messenger*. But over time, through the intertestamental period, the terminology for heavenly beings was refined. Names like *cherubim*, *seraphim*, *sons of God*, and *hosts* were often simplified or reclassified under one general term: *angel*.

By the time Jesus spoke in the New Testament, this word had become the standard label for Heaven's emissaries. And He embraced it.

But more striking than the word He used was how He used it: always in the plural. That detail matters. Because repetition in Scripture is rarely without purpose. When Jesus used the plural "angels" every single time, He was pointing to something more than just heavenly traffic.

He was announcing a new framework of collaboration, a collective heavenly engagement that would coincide with the

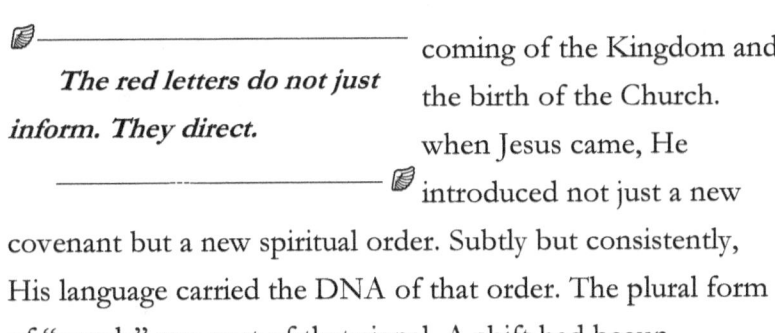

The red letters do not just inform. They direct.

coming of the Kingdom and the birth of the Church. when Jesus came, He introduced not just a new covenant but a new spiritual order. Subtly but consistently, His language carried the DNA of that order. The plural form of "angels" was part of that signal. A shift had begun.

Why Red Letters Matter

Before we explore the implications of that plural form, we need to take one more step: understanding why Jesus' words, *specifically* His words, deserve this level of focused attention.

You may be familiar with red-letter Bibles, where the words of Jesus appear in red (or sometimes blue). This isn't just a typographic flourish. It reflects a deep spiritual conviction: the words of Jesus Christ, the incarnate Word, hold a unique and central authority in the Christian faith. Even if we hold different views about how inspiration works or how exact translations might be, we can agree that what Jesus said, and how He said it, matters deeply. Whether, we are exploring questions of theology, ethics, or the mysteries of Heaven, the red-letter words of Jesus form a compass. They are the grounding source for how we interpret all other truths. And that's why this book places such weight on His use of the plural. Not because the rest of Scripture is less

The Gate of Number

inspired, but because Jesus' exact phrases, rhythms, and choices carry the heart of Heaven into human speech.

Consider just a few examples:

Matthew 13:41, 16:27, 24:31, 25:31, 26:53, Mark 8:38, 13:27, Luke 9:26, 12:8–9, 15:10, 16:22, John 1:51. In every single case, Jesus uses "angels." Always plural. Never singular.

This is not accidental. This is a gate.

Why Plural Form Matters Spiritually

Now we can return to the plural form itself, with a fresh understanding of why it matters. Plural is part, in grammar, to the larger category of "number" which includes singular (and in Hebrew, also dual). But it is a category that tells us even more, both materially and spiritually.

Plural can mean:

- Quantity (many rather than one)

- Indefiniteness (not specified, not limited)

- Diversity (variety in nature or function)

- Collectivity (a unified group, like the Church or the Host of Heaven)

Light on the Number

- Majesty or greatness, as in the *Pluralis Excellentiae*, a reverent form used in Hebrew to elevate the dignity of a person or being

When Jesus used the plural "angels," He may have been invoking all of these layers at once. We'll explore them in depth shortly but know this: the plural isn't just about numbers. It's about meaning, *majesty*, and mission.

> **The plural form doesn't count Angels. It reveals their majesty and mission.**

STARS: WHERE NUMBER MEETS THE SPIRITUAL

To illustrate how deeply embedded number is in God's revelation, we turn to a vivid and often-overlooked biblical symbol: stars. The most popular fascination about stars in astronomy relates to their numbers. In Scripture, stars serve as a bridge between the physical and the spiritual. They are literal, visible creations, but they are also spiritual metaphors, often representing heavenly beings.

When God spoke to Abraham in Genesis 15:5–6, He said:

"Look up at the sky and count the stars, if indeed you can count them." Then he said to him, "So shall your offspring be."

The Gate of Number

This was not just about population. It was a prophetic image, linking heavenly quantity to earthly destiny.

Psalm 147 deepens the mystery:

"He telleth the number of the stars; He calleth them all by name."

And Isaiah 45:12 declares:

"My hands stretched out the heavens, and with My breath I established all their starry host."

> *In God's world, number is not random-it is revelation.*

In these passages, "number" is sacred. It signals God's sovereignty, intentionality, and knowledge. When Jesus uses the plural "angels," He echoes this tradition. He draws our attention to the Heavenly Host, not as an abstraction, but as a numbered, named, and active force.

The Four Dimensions of the Number Gate

From all of this, four major insights emerge, core dimensions that this book will unfold:

1. Reverence – Rooted in the *Pluralis Excellentiae*, showing awe for the greatness of God's spiritual order.

   > **The plural is not grammatical-it is glorious.**

2. Collective Identity – A salient implication of plural at the crossroads of language use and social dynamics. It shows that Angels appear as a unified, purposeful company; likewise, we are called to operate in spiritual community.

3. Quantity – The first and most common reference of the category of number. It shows us that Heaven is not sparse. God's provision is abundant, His army countless.

4. Complexity – The plural reveals diversity and design, each Angels unique, each role precise, every movement orchestrated.

These four insights are not just theological curiosities. They are revelations of the gate into how we perceive Heaven, and how we are meant to live as spiritual people in collaboration with it.

And So We Begin

The plural was not just grammar. It was glory.

The Gate of Number

A signal. A strategy. A spiritual shift.

And Jesus, by choosing it, opened something profound.

A gate for us to enter.

Let us walk through.

The Number of Reverence

The seraphim stood above him. Each had six wings: with two he covered his face, and with two he covered his feet, and with two he was flying. They kept on calling to each other: "Holy, holy, holy is the LORD of the Heavenly Armies! The whole earth is full of his glory! **Isaiah 6:2-3**

In Chapter 1, we uncover the first divine signal that opens the gate to understanding the Hosts of Heaven: *reverence*. Drawing from Jesus' exclusive use of the plural when referring to Angels, we explore the spiritual depth of the pluralis excellentiae—a grammatical form used in Hebrew not to count, but to glorify. Jesus' words reveal a posture, not just a point: reverence is the atmosphere of Heaven. It is how He sees the Angels, and how He invites us to see them. More than a linguistic insight, this chapter lays the first spiritual foundation for collaboration with the Heavenly Host. Through Jesus' reverent tone, we are called to realign our language, our view, and our spiritual culture to Heaven's decorum. This is the first step toward interaction with Angels—and the first step toward fulfilling our shared commission with them.

CHAPTER I

THE NUMBER OF REVERENCE.

WHEN PLURAL MEANS GLORY

Imagine hearing a word that, though plural in form, refers to only one being, and does so with majestic intensity. It's a linguistic paradox that opens a spiritual window. In the Hebrew Scriptures, this phenomenon is known as the *pluralis excellentiae*, the "plural of excellence" or "majestic plural." It doesn't indicate multiple entities. Instead, it magnifies greatness. It elevates glory.

This form is more than a grammatical curiosity. It is a vessel of reverence, reserved for sacred use in

> *Jesus used the plural not by habit, but by holy design.*

the language of Heaven's people. While other cultures occasionally use a "royal we," ancient Hebrew developed a nuanced and deliberate way to signal spiritual exaltation through language. The *pluralis excellentiae* is used for God, for His attributes, and for the most awe-filled realities of the unseen realm. It speaks not just to identity, but to honor. And this is where we step into holy ground: Jesus Himself uses the plural, exclusively, when referring to Angels. Not once does He revert to a singular. This is not accidental. It is intentional.

The Gate of Number

His speech is shaped by the sacred linguistic patterns of the Hebrew Scriptures, and every word is chosen with spiritual weight.

Jesus knows exactly what this usage signals.

He is speaking from within a linguistic and theological tradition that saturates meaning into every syllable, especially when referencing the divine or the angelic. And His listeners, trained in that tradition, would not miss the signal. They would hear the plural and feel its pull. They would recognize the pattern used for Elohim, for Adonai, and now, for the Hosts of Heaven.

To them, this plural wasn't merely numerical. It was revelatory.

It revealed that Angels, in the mind of the Messiah, were not only numerous but majestic, not only active, but exalted. He was inviting them to see what He saw: the Angels not as background figures, but as dignified agents of Heaven's will.

This is how the insight emerged. His consistent use of the plural, without exception, prompted the question: *Why?* Why insist on the plural unless it was meant to teach something? The answer, rooted in both Scripture and Jesus' cultural-linguistic context, is that this form carried an unmissable message. A message His hearers were prepared to recognize: these beings, these Angels, are to be regarded with reverence.

The Number of Reverence

> *The plural was Heaven's grammar-and Jesus spoke it fluently.*

So this plural becomes our first threshold. A gate. A key to revelation.

It is not merely a matter of grammar. It is a matter of glory. And through it, Jesus begins to unfold the divine decorum of Heaven, a world in which reverence flows between Creator and Host, and where humans are invited to align with this holy order.

Let us step further into what He meant us to see.

From Hebrew Roots to Global Reach

To understand the weight of Jesus' words, we must begin with this: His voice rose from within the house of Israel. Though our record of His words comes to us in Koine Greek, the rhythm and depth behind them were shaped by the Hebrew mind, and echo through a people entrusted with the oracles of God (Romans 3:2).

Koine Greek, the common dialect of the Roman world, was the bridge-language of empires. It was born from the conquests of Alexander the Great and refined across the diverse cultures of the Mediterranean. Accessible and practical, it carried trade, law, and philosophy from Greece to Egypt, Judea, and beyond. It is the language in which the

The Gate of Number

New Testament would be written, so the Good News could be proclaimed from Jerusalem to the nations.

But Jesus' spiritual and linguistic formation was first and foremost Jewish.

He likely spoke Aramaic, the everyday dialect of Judea. But He also understood and operated within the linguistic sanctity of Hebrew, especially in the way He framed sacred realities. This explains why, even when His words were later recorded in Greek, they retained unmistakable echoes of the Hebraic worldview, and of the Scriptural tradition in which He stood.

Jesus knew the *pluralis excellentiae*. He came from the people who used it to honor God. He drew on its majesty when He referred to Angels. And He did so knowing that His Jewish audience would grasp the signal.

This is why the insight carries weight. It is not something we are inventing backward from modern interpretation. Rather, it is a thread sewn forward by Jesus Himself; one He knew would resonate with those trained to listen. They were people who had recited the Psalms, who had heard the Torah sung aloud, who understood that plurals in Hebrew could mean more than number, they could mean glory.

And so, even though the New Testament comes to us in Greek, the heartbeat beneath the words is Hebrew. That heartbeat is reverence. And reverence does not get lost in translation.

Jesus spoke into a cultural and theological framework that honored the sacred texture of language. When He spoke of Angels, He chose reverence, even in grammar.

> *The plural was Heaven's grammar-and Jesus spoke it fluently.*

And He expected His listeners, shaped by the same Scriptures, to understand the revelation encoded in His words.

This is why we must pay attention, not just to what He said, but how He said it. In the folds of His syntax was the whisper of Heaven.

Let us now return to that sacred tongue and examine how the *pluralis excellentiae* speaks, so that we, too, may hear what He meant us to catch.

When Language Bows: The Hebrew Grammar of Majesty

To better grasp the weight of Jesus' use of the plural when referring to Angels, we must first understand that He

The Gate of Number

was drawing from a known pattern, a pattern that was already deeply woven into the Hebrew Scriptures. His choice was not innovative; it was rooted in reverent tradition. And to see that clearly, we need to look at the examples that form the foundation of this usage.

The most prominent and undeniable case is the name אֱלֹהִים (*Elohim*), one of the most frequent titles for God in the Hebrew Bible. Though plural in form, it is nearly always used with singular verbs and adjectives when referring to the one true God. This is seen clearly in the very first verse of the Bible:

"...בְּרֵאשִׁית בָּרָא אֱלֹהִים"

"In the beginning, *Elohim* created the heavens and the earth" (Genesis 1:1, TS2009).

The verb "created" (*bara*) is singular. This pairing of a plural subject with a singular verb is not a grammatical mistake. It is an intentional declaration of exalted majesty, a plural used not for number, but for glory.

Another familiar example is the word אֲדֹנָי (*Adonai*), often translated as "Lord." Though it literally means "lords" or "masters," it is used as a reverent name for God, and always treated as a singular being. In Psalm 136:2, we read:

"Give thanks to the God (*Adonai*) of gods (*Elohim*), for He is good…"

The Number of Reverence

Here again, plural forms are used to point not to multiplicity, but to divine supremacy.

But this reverent usage doesn't stop with God. The pluralis excellentiae also appears in reference to exceptional beings who serve in God's presence.

- The word קדֹשׁים (*Qedoshim*), meaning "Holy Ones," can refer to both God and the Angels. Its plural form communicates not just moral purity, but heavenly elevation.

- In Isaiah 6:3, we hear the Seraphim cry:

- "Holy, holy, holy is the Lord of Hosts…"

- The thrice-repeated "holy" (*kadosh*) intensifies this sense of unapproachable majesty. These "Holy Ones" do not speak casually. Their speech mirrors the reverence embedded in the very grammar of Heaven.

Two more examples underscore this same pattern:

- Seraphim – derived from *saraph*, meaning "to burn." Though plural, it often refers to a unique class of exalted Angel whose fiery nature expresses God's purifying glory.

The Gate of Number

- Cherubim – from *keruv*, this plural form refers to another class of Angelic being, often seen guarding sacred space or the throne of God. Even when singular in reference, the plural form is used to heighten their majesty.

Translation may veil, but reverence never vanishes.

In all of these, the "-im" plural ending is not about number. It's about weight. The kind of weight that demands reverence.

The consistent use of the pluralis excellentiae throughout Hebrew Scripture shows that this is not a passing grammatical style. It is a sacred linguistic strategy, one that distinguishes beings who are set apart, exalted, and filled with glory. Jesus, shaped by this linguistic tradition, knew exactly what He was doing when He used this form to refer to Angels.

Before we turn to how this usage moves into the Greek Scriptures, and where its nuances begin to blur, we must carry with us this realization: Jesus was not breaking with tradition. He was honoring it. And through it, He was inviting us to see the Heavenly Host as Heaven sees them, not merely numerous, but noble.

Reverence Across Tongues: What Translation Can't Hide

The pluralis excellentiae is a treasure of Hebrew thought, a form shaped in the sacred soil of Israel's covenant language. But as the Scriptures moved beyond Hebrew borders, carried on the wings of translation, some of its mystery grew quieter. Not lost, only veiled.

This unique grammatical form, used to elevate the majestic and the holy, does not translate easily. Each language reflects a different worldview. And in the case of Hebrew and Greek, that difference is profound. Hebrew breathes reverence even in its grammar; Greek, by contrast, pursues clarity and order. And so, when the Hebrew Scriptures were translated into Koine Greek, the Septuagint (LXX), some of Heaven's thunder was thinned into rain.

Take the divine name Elohim. In Hebrew, it is plural in form but singular in usage, used almost 2,600 times to refer to the one true God. In the Septuagint, it is most often rendered as κύριος (*Kyrios*), "Lord." The word is singular. Precise. Functional. It names God rightly, but cannot carry the layered majesty that Elohim does.

Yet even the Greek translators knew that sometimes, one "Lord" was not enough. In places like Psalm 50:1, the translators reached for the plural:

The Gate of Number

"οἱ θεοὶ, οἱ θεοὶ ἐφώνησαν", "the gods, the gods have called."

Here, the Hebrew has a form that reflects divine grandeur, not polytheism, but plurality for the sake of reverence. The LXX mirrors that by using plural θεοὶ (*theoi*), showing that even Greek sometimes had to bend its norms to capture Heaven's weight.

Still, these are exceptions. The Greek language, and later the New Testament itself, typically moves toward grammatical simplicity and theological precision. Early Christian writers, wanting to affirm the oneness of God in a Greco-Roman world filled with gods, defaulted to singular forms for God. The pluralis excellentiae all but disappears in visible form, though it still whispers in the background.

And yet, Jesus' usage stands apart.

He does not use the singular when referring to Angels. Not once. He consistently says "the Angels," in the plural. In Greek. In public. In teaching. Even though He had no external reason to do so, no grammatical obligation, no theological pressure, He chooses the plural.

Why?

Because His heart was still speaking Hebrew, even when His words were carried in Greek.

The Number of Reverence

He was drawing from the reverent grammar of Heaven, the same grammar that named Elohim and Adonai, the same plural forms that exalted the Seraphim and Cherubim. And more than that, He was revealing His roots. As the fulfillment of the Law and the Prophets, Jesus needed to show that He stood within, not outside, the Scriptural tradition. His words were not an abandonment of Hebrew reverence, but its perfect expression.

This mattered to His audience. Many of them were looking for signs of legitimacy, proof that this teacher from Galilee was not inventing a new doctrine, but fulfilling an ancient one. His choice of language was one of those signs. The plural He used was not only a signal of reverence, it was a signal of continuity.

The deeper implication is this: Jesus was not only teaching about Angels, He was honoring them. His words formed a spiritual decorum. A recognition of dignity. A witness to a heavenly reality that the grammar itself tried to uphold.

Even across languages, the reverence remained.

Translation may veil, but reverence never vanishes.

So what does this tell us?

That language can shift, but reverence endures. That grammar may be bound by culture, but glory transcends translation. And most of all, that when Jesus speaks of Angels, He does so not with detachment, but with deep familiarity and honor.

He is not simply acknowledging their presence. He is announcing their worth.

Let us listen again, this time more attentively, to the weight He gave them, and ask what that weight now calls forth from us.

Heaven's Tone: How Jesus Revealed the Reverence of God

Understanding Scripture means entering not just its words, but its worldview, its culture, its cadence, its holy assumptions. When Jesus chose the plural for Angels, He was not embellishing. He was echoing Heaven's tone.

That choice carries more than grammatical interest. It reflects the very sentiments of God.

Jesus spoke reverently of the Heavenly Hosts because God Himself is clothed in reverence. His glory is not solitary. It radiates, surrounds, and honors what He has made. This divine posture is evident in Jesus' treatment of Angels. Though He created them, through whom all things were made (John 1:3; Colossians 1:16), He does not speak of them as subordinates to be commanded, but as servants to be affirmed, as allies to be honored.

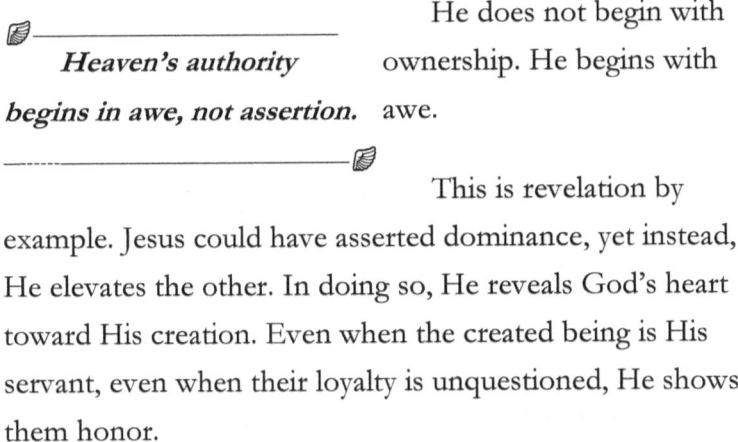

Heaven's authority begins in awe, not assertion.

He does not begin with ownership. He begins with awe.

This is revelation by example. Jesus could have asserted dominance, yet instead, He elevates the other. In doing so, He reveals God's heart toward His creation. Even when the created being is His servant, even when their loyalty is unquestioned, He shows them honor.

This tells us much about the kind of King He is.

It also speaks to the atmosphere of Heaven. Reverence is not reserved only for God; it flows from Him and fills His House. In this House, language, posture, and tone align with holy dignity. That's what Jesus embodied. And that is what He invites us to share.

This posture is not only divine. It is also deeply human.

Jesus lived under the weight of human limitations. His flesh could be tired, hungry, tempted, and worn. He was subject to the very weaknesses we know well. And yet, even in that vulnerability, He did not try to prove Himself by resisting or rivaling the Angels. He did not resent their

The Gate of Number

strength or glory. He welcomed their assistance. He blessed their activity.

Reverence became the atmosphere in which He collaborated with them, not as a backup plan, but as a model for how Heaven works on Earth.

And so, Jesus becomes for us the perfect bridge: as God, He honors the Hosts He made; as Man, He demonstrates how to walk with them humbly. In both, He shows us how to live in step with Heaven's character.

We would do well to notice the tone He chose.

His reverence was not cold formality. It was saturated with:

- Humility: aware of glory without grasping for it

- Appreciation: recognizing another's faithful service

- Affirmation: giving dignity where it is due

- Honor: publicly and privately

- Love: not only for humanity, but for Heaven

These attitudes form more than a list. They form an environment, an invisible atmosphere in which Angels feel welcome, trusted, and respected.

And the Angels noticed.

They are the most attentive audience in creation. Ever watchful, ever responsive to Heaven's alignment, they would have perceived Jesus' posture toward them. They would have heard it in His voice. They would have seen it in His choices. And they would have responded, not just with obedience, but with praise. *Holy!*

Reverence creates atmosphere. And Angels fill it.

This may help explain why Angels are so overwhelmingly present in the Gospel accounts. From His conception to His resurrection, and even at His return, their nearness testifies to more than divine strategy. It speaks of divine atmosphere. Where there is reverence, there is room for Angels.

And that raises the question: what does our language make room for?

If Jesus used words that invited Angels, honored them, and created an atmosphere of collaboration, then our words must do the same. If we are to walk with the Hosts of Heaven in fulfilling God's purpose on earth, we must first adopt the tone of Heaven. And Jesus has shown us how.

Let us begin to speak as He spoke, with reverence, alignment, and readiness for holy partnership.

Reverence Is the Atmosphere of Heaven

If Jesus revealed reverence in how He spoke of Angels, then we must ask: *Where did He get it from?* What is the spiritual climate from which that reverence flows?

We find a glimpse in Psalm 89, a majestic window into the unseen realm. There, the psalmist describes a scene not on Earth, but in the divine assembly, that radiant council of the Heavenly Hosts who surround the throne of God.

In the King James Version, the psalm reads:

"God is greatly to be feared in the assembly of the saints, and to be had in reverence of all them that are about him." (Psalm 89:7 KJV)

And in the TS2009 version, the same passage offers a richer Hebrew echo:

"El is greatly feared in the company of the set-apart ones, and awesome above all those around Him." (Psalm 89:7 TS2009)

This is not metaphor. It is revelation.

What the psalmist sees is not just a gathering, but a cosmic reality, a divine culture. Around God are beings called "set-apart ones" or "saints," a term often used for Heavenly Hosts. And in their midst, reverence is the norm. Awe is not requested, it is present. It surrounds Him like light. It defines the behavior of those nearest to Him.

And notice how many names for God are used in just a few verses: El, Yah, Yehôvah, Elohim. This multiplication of titles is not poetic excess. It reflects the multifaceted revelation of God's nature, as seen by those who behold Him directly.

The same vision appears again in Psalm 82:1:

"God stands in the congregation of the mighty; He judges among the gods." (KJV)

Or in the TS2009:

"Elohim stands in the congregation of El; He judges in the midst of the elohim."

Here, God is pictured among a council of heavenly beings who themselves carry divine resemblance. So glorious are they that the psalmist risks confusion. Who is Elohim? Who is El? Who are these other *elohim*? This is not polytheism. It is divine honor granted to created beings who serve in the presence of their Creator.

Heaven is not insecure about majesty.

God does not diminish His servants to make Himself greater. He elevates them. He honors them. He sits among

The Gate of Number

them. And in doing so, He invites the observer to learn: what makes Him truly holy is not that He hoards glory, but that He shares it.

This is the culture Jesus came from.

And it is the culture He carried with Him into the earth.

His way of speaking of Angels is the same culture reflected here: God among His Host, reverent of His own creation, not ashamed to dwell among those He has exalted.

This should give us pause. We often struggle to honor even our fellow humans. Yet God Himself sits in counsel with His Hosts and allows Himself to be surrounded by glory so similar to His own that only spiritual discernment can distinguish Him. As the psalmist pleads in Psalm 82:8:

"Arise, O God, judge the earth: for thou shalt inherit all nations."

It is the same theme we see in Jesus. When Peter declared, *"You are the Christ, the Son of the living God,"* Jesus did not credit logic or deduction. He said,

"Flesh and blood has not revealed this to you, but My Father in heaven." (Matthew 16:17)

In Heaven, reverence and resemblance walk together. The closer one gets to the presence of God, the more honor flows outward, not just upward. That is the signature of divine culture.

And this, too, is the tone Jesus modeled.

His reverence for Angels was not mere politeness. It was the decorum of Heaven, worn on Earth. It is the attitude sung by Mary in her Magnificat, the song that speaks of how God:

- "Regarded the low estate of His handmaiden"
- "Scattered the proud"
- "Put down the mighty"
- "Exalted them of low degree"
- "Filled the hungry with good things"
- "Remembered mercy"
- (Luke 1:48–54)

Heaven honors. And it does so without hesitation.

In this way, reverence becomes more than a virtue. It becomes a lens, a way of seeing others, a way of speaking, a way of judging, a way of aligning with Heaven. If we do not learn to speak with reverence, we will misname what God is honoring. And if we do not recognize reverence as the language of Heaven, we may resist what God is drawing near.

Let us ask: Where does reverence dwell in our speech, our relationships, our worship? For in Heaven's atmosphere, only reverence can breathe.

REVERENT EYES: THE FIRST GATE INTO THE HEAVENLY WORLD

The way we see determines the way we walk.

And the way we see Heaven, its order, its Agents, its majesty, depends on the lenses we've adopted. Some lenses are inherited through culture. Others are formed through our theology. But all of us live and move within an internal framework, a way of perceiving that shapes how we respond to what is unseen.

This chapter has not simply revealed a grammatical detail. It has exposed a lens. A spiritual lens that Jesus Himself wore, a lens of reverence.

When He spoke of Angels, He didn't use the plural casually. He used it consistently, intentionally, and with an awareness of

> *Jesus didn't just name Angels-He enthroned them in our imagination.*

the revelation it carried. He was not merely identifying the

The Number of Reverence

Angels. He was positioning them, in the spiritual imagination of His listeners, and now, in ours.

And by doing so, He was inviting us to see what He sees.

When Jesus uses language shaped by the Hebrew Scriptures, language soaked in reverence and awe, He's not decorating His speech. He's opening a gate. He's saying, *"Look again. This is not poetry. This is Heaven."*

And if Heaven is filled with reverence, then so must we be, if we are to walk with it, hear it, and partner with its Hosts.

This is why lenses matter.

If we look at Angels and see only symbolic messengers, or distant mythic figures, then we will miss their nearness, their dignity, and their place in God's plan. If we see them as tools and not as trustworthy beings, we will speak wrongly, act rashly, or dismiss the very ones sent to help us.

But if we take on the lenses Jesus used, the lenses of reverence, we begin to see rightly. We begin to recognize the Heavenly Host as God's faithful collaborators, not only around His throne, but among us, aiding the fulfillment of His will on Earth.

The Gate of Number

> **Reverence is not delay. It's the doorway.**

We begin to see that reverence is not a pause before action. It is the first action, the atmosphere that invites alignment.

And that alignment opens the gate to relationship.

That's what Jesus was doing. He was not just teaching *about* Angels. He was showing us how to live with them. With honor. With recognition. With readiness.

This is the first unveiling. The first turning of the lock.

From here, we will go deeper. We will explore what reverence births: recognition, collaboration, and ultimately, commission. For the Hosts of Heaven are not only glorious, they are assigned. And so are we.

But before we can walk with Angels, we must learn to see them rightly.

Jesus has shown us how.

> **We cannot walk with the Host of Heaven until we see them with reverent eyes**

Let us now walk through this gate, with reverent eyes, and with hearts ready for the journey ahead.

Chapter 1
To Meditate Further

1. How does my language reflect my view of the unseen spiritual world?

2. What would it look like to practice reverence in my daily spiritual rhythm?

3. How can I train my heart to perceive Angels with the same honor Jesus showed?

4. Where have I allowed familiarity or spiritual casualness to dim my awe of Heaven?

5. In what ways can reverence become the culture of my home, church, or leadership?

(Hebrews 12:28; Psalm 89:7; Luke 12:8–9; Daniel 10:5–12; Isaiah 6:1–5; Exodus 3:5; Matthew 12:36)

The Gate of Number

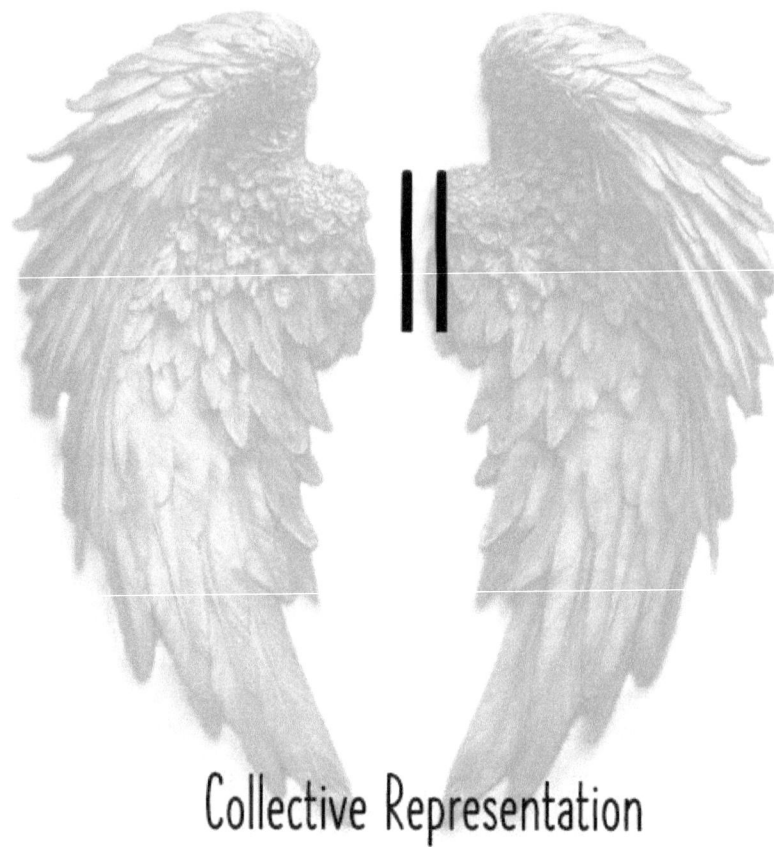

Collective Representation

That they all may be one; as thou, Father, art in me, and I in thee, that they also may be one in us... I in them, and thou in me, that they may be made perfect in one. **John 17:21–23**

Jesus' consistent use of the plural form when referring to Angels reveals more than number—it unveils a divine pattern of unity, purpose, and shared identity. This chapter explores the cultural, linguistic, and theological significance of that choice, uncovering a rich insight: the Angels do not act alone but represent Heaven as a coordinated and collective force. Their representation becomes a mirror for the Church, which is likewise called to function in unity—not as isolated individuals, but as one body, working with and alongside the Heavenly Hosts. Drawing from biblical language, ancient cultural expressions, and even illustrations from nature, this chapter calls readers to embrace the divine wisdom embedded in collectivity. The path to collaboration with Angels begins not with personal strength, but with alignment to a corporate identity—a family joined in purpose, governed by Heaven's order, and summoned to act together in fulfilling the Great Commission. ¶

CHAPTER 2

COLLECTIVE REPRESENTATION

WHEN SILENCE SPEAKS

The words that come from the mouth of Jesus may appear simple, even straightforward for some. They offer peace, like a still breeze that carries the scent of eternity. For others, they seem obscure, even disorienting, disconnected from logic or difficult to grasp. And to still others, they may seem so ordinary that they miss the sacred weight entirely.

But whatever impression they leave, one thing remains constant: they are Truth.

Jesus' words are not casual. They are crafted to draw the seeker deeper, to awaken intimacy with God, and to uncover the listener's divine purpose. Their power is not limited to immediate clarity; they invite exploration. The responsibility to discern their depth rests not on the speaker, but on the one who hears. The hearer must rise to the level of the word, must lean in, must receive.

This is especially true of Jesus' linguistic choices. The structure of His speech, the forms He uses, and even the categories of grammar He employs are part of His divine communication. Every pattern, every silence, every repetition is filled with purpose. His exclusive use of the plural when speaking of Angels, for instance, does not end with the majestic implications explored in the "Pluralis Excellentiae." There is more; something equally profound, but quieter. Something hidden not just in what He says, but in what He consistently chooses not to say.

This is where we begin the second insight: the revelation of Collective Representation.

Jesus never refers to Angels in the singular, not once. He never speaks of "an Angel" detached from others. Even when the scene or grammar might allow for it, He holds to the plural. This pattern invites us to ask: *What is He showing us through what He omits?*

> *Jesus never said "an Angel." He said "the Angels"-and that speaks volumes.*

The answer is found in Scripture itself, where we repeatedly encounter Angels in unity, functioning as a singular chorus with a shared identity and mission. Revelation 5:11 describes "the voice of many Angels," numbering in the tens of thousands, all encircling the throne. In Hebrews 12:22, believers are welcomed into the company of "innumerable Angels in joyful assembly." And in Luke 2:13, a multitude of the Heavenly Host suddenly appears, not to deliver scattered messages, but to worship as one.

These are not simply large groups. They are unified formations. Their actions do not reveal individuality in isolation, but collective harmony and mutual representation.

This principle is not limited to theology. It finds echoes in the fields of linguistics and social psychology, where groups are often treated as singular agents. We speak of nations, councils, families, and communities as if they are single bodies, because they act with collective intention, carry shared authority, and represent a larger identity than the sum of their parts.

Jesus, with divine precision, taps into this sacred logic. His use of the plural does more than honor majesty, it introduces the structure of Heaven. It teaches us that Angels are not freelancers of the spirit realm. They are members of a corporate order, defined not only by function, but by unity.

Angels do not freelance. They function as a family.

In the pages ahead, I will briefly draw from a few human disciplines to illuminate how this dynamic works, how individuals relate to their collective identity, and how this may help us understand the Heavenly Hosts, not just as glorious beings, but as participants in a shared mission.

Collective Representation

These technical reflections will be brief. They may seem abstract at first glance, but I trust they will cast helpful light on the deeper design we are invited to see. Because what Jesus didn't say matters just as much as what He did.

THE HEAVENLY LOGIC OF COLLECTIVE IDENTITY

To fully grasp the revelation embedded in Jesus' consistent use of the plural when speaking of Angels, we must step briefly into the world of language, culture, and shared consciousness. For behind the grammar lies a divine pattern, what scholars in social psychology and the humanities call collective representation.

This concept refers to the way individuals act, speak, and live not merely as isolated selves, but as members of a body, as living expressions of the identity and values of a larger whole. In this view, the "I" is shaped by the "we," and every personal action carries the fragrance of collective purpose.

When Jesus speaks of Angels only in the plural, He is not simply using a formal or traditional term. He is unveiling a deeper principle:

Heaven's grammar carries Heaven's order.

that Angels do not operate as autonomous agents, but as coordinated representatives of Heaven's collective will. His

The Gate of Number

grammar reveals more than reverence, it reveals structure, order, and belonging.

This understanding becomes even clearer when we observe how language itself carries the weight of such concepts. Many languages possess built-in ways of expressing collective nuance. A well-known example is the distinction between inclusive and exclusive plurals. In some cultures, the word *we* can mean "you and I" (inclusive), or "they and I, but not you" (exclusive). These fine distinctions are not superficial; they reflect the deep social dynamics within a culture.

Beyond grammar, collective representation finds voice in traditions, rituals, and shared stories. In any people group, plural forms are not merely about numbers; they become carriers of memory, identity, and covenant. In Scripture, this principle shines with divine clarity: the Hosts of Heaven are never portrayed as scattered actors, but as a unified multitude, moving as one body, praising as one choir, sent as one army.

Jesus lived and taught in this world. The Aramaic language, commonly spoken in His time, was rich with communal awareness. Its plural forms carried far more than numerical value, they carried the weight of belonging, of shared participation. The people who listened to Jesus would have

> **To ancient ears, His plural was a signal-heard in Heaven's accent.**

instinctively understood His choice of plural not as grammatical accident, but as a theological signal: that Angels belong to one another, act as one, and exist within a holy ecosystem of interdependence.

Greek, the language in which His words would later be recorded, also allowed for expressing this depth. Though shaped by a more individualistic worldview, Koine Greek retained tools for showing collective dynamics, especially through its use of definite articles and flexible modifiers. So, when the Gospel writers preserved Jesus' plural references to Angels, the force of that collectivity remained intact.

And the Scriptures are rich with examples. When Jesus speaks of "the holy Angels" who will accompany the Son of Man (Mark 8:38), or of "His Angels" sent to execute judgment (Matthew 13:41), we hear inclusive plurals, those who work with Him, aligned with His glory. When He speaks of "twelve legions of Angels" ready to defend Him (Matthew 26:53), or of humanity becoming "like the Angels in Heaven" (Matthew 22:30), He uses exclusive plurals, distinguishing between human and Angelic roles, yet never denying the honor or proximity of either. And yet, even with these distinctions available to Him, Jesus rarely insists on them. His words consistently preserve the collective identity of Angels, without separating them into ranks or emphasizing difference. In doing so, He reinforces Heaven's message: that to serve God is to belong to a divine order, where individuality does not vanish, but is fulfilled through unity.

How Plural Language Reveals Kingdom Alignment

The Trinity: Heaven's First Community

Representation as the Rhythm of Heaven and Earth

To represent is never a solitary act. It is to carry something greater than oneself, to stand, speak, or act on behalf of another. Representation means you were sent from within a larger order, entrusted with its voice, its values, and its purpose.

This is what makes the Hosts of Heaven so revelatory. They do not operate in isolation. They do not pursue personal assignments. They are participants in a shared purpose, moving in rhythm with the will of the One who sends them. Whether appearing in vision, releasing messages, protecting the righteous, or executing judgment, they always act in concert with divine intention.

They are not random messengers. They are representatives.

Angels don't just show up. They represent.

Every Angel we encounter in Scripture speaks not merely for God, but from God, as one woven into the order of Heaven. They reflect the logic of representation, which always assumes two truths: there is One who sends, and there is a community being represented. The Angel is never just one. The Angel is always from the Many, on behalf of the One.

This same principle is embedded in the Church.

We were never meant to walk alone in divine mission. Our calling is not to individual greatness but to corporate obedience, to reflect Heaven's unity through earthly collaboration. The Body of Christ is not a loose collection of saved souls. It is a system of representational grace, where each part carries something for the whole.

The Angelic realm teaches us how this works.

Heavenly authority flows from divine proximity-and holy alignment.

Angels move in alignment. They do not compete for glory or isolate themselves in private assignments. Their authority flows from proximity to God, but also from alignment with

The Gate of Number

one another. They model a Kingdom where order is not control, but cooperation. Where mission is not self-initiated, but received and shared. Where identity is not detached but deeply embedded in collective loyalty.

This is the atmosphere of Heaven.

And Earth is meant to reflect it.

To live apart from this order is to live in disconnection, from Heaven, from the Body, and often from the mission itself. But to enter into this flow is to become, like the Angels, a sent one, not just called, but commissioned; not just inspired, but in step.

Representation is not about status. It is about trust. About carrying something sacred not as your own, but as one who has been drawn into a greater communion.

This is how Heaven governs. And this is how we must learn to serve.

We Belong to the Family of Heaven

The individual believer will remember this: you do not stand alone.

From the beginning, God has never intended that we live, minister, or carry our calling in isolation. The patterns of Heaven declare it. The speech of Jesus confirms it. The unity of the Angelic Host reveals it. The believer, no matter how personally gifted or spiritually aware, is called to represent, not to replace. To belong, not to compete. To serve from within, not apart.

> *In Heaven's family, we don't compete-we represent.*

This chapter has gently shifted our lens. What began as a grammatical observation has opened into a revelation: that identity in the Kingdom is always relational. Angels never act as isolated figures. They speak from within the system of Heaven. They move in divine formation. And Jesus, with consistent reverence, honors that formation with every word He speaks.

So it is with the Church.

The Church is more than a congregation of redeemed individuals. It is a representational body, called to act in harmony, to reflect the pattern of Heaven, to walk in unity without losing uniqueness. In the Heavenly Host we see not only glory, but cooperation. Not only holiness, but order. Not only majesty, but alignment. These are not just heavenly principles, they are our pattern.

When the Body of Christ forgets this, we fracture into silos, each gift isolated, each ministry self-contained, each assignment burdened by the weight of aloneness. But Heaven teaches us differently. Heaven invites us into a rhythm of shared movement. It teaches us to speak and serve and walk as one, even while remaining many.

We are not self-sent. We are not self-owned. We are not alone. Heaven has a family. And we are called to live as those who belong to it.

The Angelic Host and the Body of Christ move according to the same spiritual principle: representation born from communion. We are trusted not because we stand apart, but because we stand together, under Christ, in reverence, for the glory of the Father, in step with the Hosts of Heaven.

To live like this is to prepare ourselves for collaboration with the unseen, for partnership with the Angelic, and for the fulfillment of the mission that Jesus entrusted to us. For the Great Commission will not be completed by scattered champions, but by aligned disciples who understand that no one walks alone.

Chapter 2
To Meditate Further

1. How does the plural form Jesus used for Angels reshape my understanding of divine unity?

2. Do I live as if I'm representing just myself—or as part of something greater?

3. What personal habits or mindsets are resisting collective purpose and identity?

4. Who are the people I'm meant to walk in unity with for this season of purpose?

5. How can I honor and embody Heaven's principle of representation in my ministry or calling?

(Psalm 133:1; Amos 3:3; John 17:21–23; Philippians 2:1–4; Hebrews 12:22–24; Romans 12:4–5; Matthew 10:40–42)

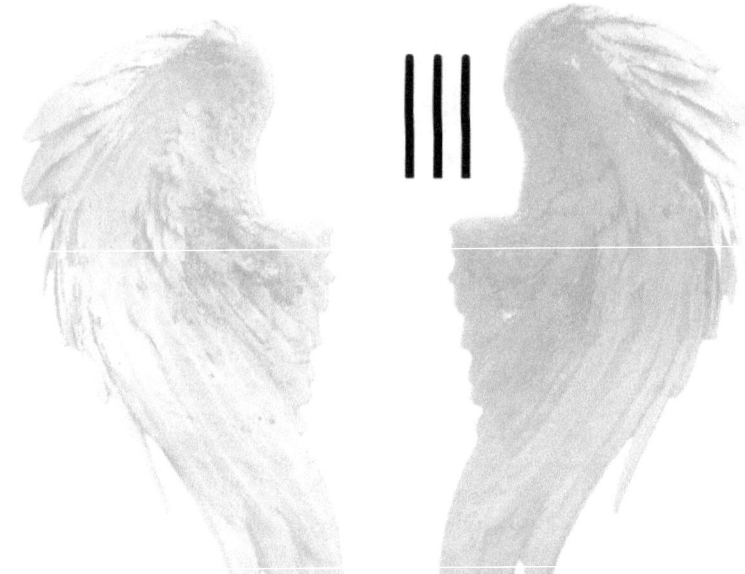

The Number of a Multitude

Fear not: for they that be with us are more than they that be with them... and, behold, the mountain was full of horses and chariots of fire round about Elisha. **2 Kings 6:16–17**

In Chapter 3, we are invited to contemplate the astonishing scale of the Heavenly Host. Jesus' consistent use of the plural-"Angels"-signals more than reverence; it unveils the vastness of Heaven's army. Drawing from the language of Revelation and other Scriptures, this chapter shows that God's Angelic Host is not a symbolic metaphor, but a structured, innumerable company: thousands upon thousands, myriads of myriads. Drawing a bridge between scientific wonder and biblical revelation, the chapter explores parallels with Carl Sagan's awe over the stars, only to reveal that the biblical witness goes even further. The Hosts are more than many-they are ready, personal, and positioned. This revelation is not just meant to inspire awe-it is meant to bring assurance. To know that we are surrounded is to walk in peace, courage, and divine confidence. The multitude is not distant: it moves with us, aligned with the Great Commission and Heaven's ongoing purposes.

CHAPTER 3

THE NUMBER OF A MULTITUDE

A WORD THAT HOLDS A WORLD

In the previous chapter, we explored how the collective identity of Angels reflects a powerful truth about Heaven's structure,

> *In Jesus' mouth, the plural form is not extra-it is exact.*

one rooted in unity, representation, and divine purpose. That insight now opens a further dimension of revelation: the role of number in how Jesus speaks about the Hosts.

Jesus' consistent use of the plural form when referring to Angels, never the singular, is not a small detail. It is part of the language of Heaven. It communicates more than theological reverence; it points toward the scale of God's heavenly family. We are invited to hear not just the glory of the Angelic realm, but also its immensity.

This repeated plural is more than a form, it is a signal. It alerts us that Jesus is speaking not of a solitary being, but of a collective beyond counting, an organized multitude already in motion. Through this choice, Jesus reveals that the unseen world is neither abstract nor minimal. It is vast, present, and active.

This understanding builds upon the idea of collective representation, but adds a new layer: scale. The scale of the Angelic Host is not ornamental, it is intentional. It is meant to evoke awe, but also assurance. The sheer number of the Heavenly Hosts speaks to both their glory and their availability for God's purposes, including those that concern us.

Heaven's Host is not decoration-it is deployment.

To help us comprehend the spiritual significance of such vastness, we may find it helpful to draw a parallel from a surprising source. For this next step, we will momentarily turn to one of the most iconic stories of scientific fascination with number and scale, offered by someone who, though not speaking theology, still opens a window that leads us to wonder.

In what follows, we will surf on one of the most iconic stories that ever tried to convey the unimaginable vastness of the cosmos, a story that prepares our hearts to better grasp the Heavenly multitude.

The Gate of Number

The Sagan number

Carl Edward Sagan was one of those minds deeply awestruck by numbers. His fascination is especially relevant here, as it brings us back to a compelling element of Creation already introduced in our reflections: the stars.

Sagan was not only an American astronomer of notable brilliance, but also a man whose writings reveal a deep commitment to the human journey. His intelligence, his wonder, and the compassion that quietly flows through his scientific work have earned my admiration. His most recognized contributions include his research on the possibility of extraterrestrial life and his involvement in sending the first physical messages into space, a symbol of humanity's longing to reach beyond itself.

But what truly captured Sagan's imagination was the sheer quantity of stars scattered across the universe. Though scientists had already begun the attempt to measure their number, Sagan brought to the effort something that transcended data, a kind of faith and poetic enthusiasm. His voice gave the field a resonance that touched the imagination of the broader American audience, especially during the wave of astronomical discovery sparked by the launch of Explorer I, the first interstellar spaceship.

Sagan reportedly believed that since the observable universe and the concept of stars were both well-defined,

The Number of A Multitude

> *Heaven hides its secrets in scale—not to confuse, but to awaken wonder.*

their number could be reasonably estimated. In many ways, that's a fair assumption. Yet what emerged from this effort was not precision, but wonder. Rather than narrowing things down, his work unveiled the elusiveness of the quest itself. As he pressed forward, he became known not for solving the count, but for awakening minds to the staggering scale of what could barely be grasped.

In his celebrated 1980 radio series *Cosmos*, Sagan voiced figures that left listeners in awe, "billions upon billions," or "100 billion galaxies, each containing 100 billion stars." He once offered the staggering estimate of ten sextillion. Eventually, the phrase "Sagan number" was coined, not to pin down a value, but to capture the idea of a number beyond human estimation.

It is not the only time in history that people have tried to wrap their minds around such magnitude. In the early Middle Ages, for example, there was a brief period of heightened curiosity about the number of Angels. Unlike Sagan's era, it didn't produce a rigorous or coordinated inquiry. But the very existence of such curiosity shows that humanity has long sensed that there is more beyond the veil, something immense, ordered, and alive.

Which leads me to wonder: if Sagan had turned his attention to the Angelic realm, if he had tried to calculate the company of Heaven, what number would he have coined to describe the count of Angels?

And truthfully, we haven't even started counting.

Scripture's Witness to Angelic Multitudes

The nature of Angelic quantity is simply different. Unlike material reality, where numbers correspond to visible forms and measurable structures, the scale of the Heavenly Hosts belongs to a different realm, one that does not yield to the usual tools of human estimation.

Scientific metaphors, like those explored in the previous section, may awaken awe. But when it comes to truth about the invisible, we must turn to a source, far more reliable: the Scriptures. For it is in the biblical witness that we begin to encounter the sheer scale and ordered vastness of the Angelic Host, not as myth, but as revealed reality.

Scripture does not reduce the Hosts to an object of quantification. Instead, it uses language that evokes both magnitude and mystery. The term that appears repeatedly is *"myriads of myriads"*. In Revelation 5:11, for example, we read: **"Then I looked and heard the voice of many Angels, numbering thousands upon thousands, and ten**

The Number of A Multitude

thousand times ten thousand." The Greek expression (*muriades muriadon*) paints the image of a number so great it surpasses clarity, it is, quite literally, myriads multiplied by myriads.

The Bible doesn't undercount- it overwhelms.

This is not imprecision. It is intentional abundance. In the biblical imagination, a *myriad* (from the Greek *murias*) could refer to a literal group of ten thousand, but it was often used to signal something too vast to count. The use of such a term in the book of Revelation, and its repetition across apocalyptic and prophetic texts, reveals that Heaven's order is not only majestic, but numerically overwhelming.

This language is not merely poetic. It is revelatory. It shows us that God has chosen to disclose the scale of His Angelic army in terms that defy containment. He is not withholding information; He is inviting reverence. Through the language of multitudes, the Spirit is saying, *Lift your eyes. Look again. You are not alone.*

These myriads are not a literary device. They are a theological reality, a revelation given to reshape our perspective, awaken trust, and expand our understanding of the Host that surrounds the throne and carries out the will of God.

Patmos and the Assembly Beyond Number

The Book of Revelation declares with clarity and majesty:

> *"And I beheld, and I heard the voice of many Angels round about the throne and the beasts and the elders: and the number of them was ten thousand times ten thousand, and thousands of thousands." (Revelation 5:11, KJV)*

The Hosts of Heaven form an innumerable company. This is not a poetic exaggeration; it is a reality affirmed across Scripture. Time and again, the Bible returns to this truth: Angels are not only many, but known, organized, and assigned. They do not move chaotically; they function in precise groups, serving in distinct roles according to God's will (Ezekiel 10:1–22; Isaiah 6:1–7; Jude 1:9; Hebrews 1:14). Every Angel is positioned within an ordered, responsive, and relational system.

> **Heaven doesn't improvise. Every Angel is precisely placed.**

This means that whenever the believer is permitted, even briefly, to glimpse this reality, what he sees is not only overwhelming in number, but also reassuring in purpose. These are not scattered forces. They are a holy multitude, coherent, activated, and aligned with the will of God. What does it mean, then, to know that we are surrounded by "thousands upon thousands" of such

The Number of A Multitude

beings? How might this shape our response to the challenges we face? Can we truly believe that this invisible Host is not only real, but working actively for our good?

The biblical image of a multitude is never a casual one. It is part of God's self-revelation. The Host is presented not in fragments, but in overwhelming fullness. And that fullness speaks.

In the twilight of the first century A.D., the apostle John, servant of Jesus Christ, found himself exiled on the barren island of Patmos. He was sent there, he says, because of "the word of God and the testimony about Jesus" (Revelation 1:9, ISV). Alone and punished for his faith, John embodied the suffering of many believers in his time. And yet it was in that very exile, at the edge of Roman power and in the silence of earthly isolation, that Heaven opened. God answered John's isolation with a vision of the throne, a vision not of emptiness, but of fullness. There, encircling the throne, stood the Angelic multitude. Though abandoned by man, John was shown that he was surrounded by God. This was not merely a doctrinal vision. It was personal comfort. And the comfort came not only in what he saw, but in what he heard.

Throughout Revelation, John records the sound of Heaven: the voice of Jesus, the roar of many waters, the music of harps, the thunder of the multitude. He writes:

The Gate of Number

"And His voice was as the sound of many waters." (Revelation 1:15, KJV)

"And I heard a voice from heaven, as the voice of many waters, and as the voice of great thunder…" (Revelation 14:2, KJV)

"And I heard as it were the voice of a great multitude… saying, Alleluia: for the Lord God omnipotent reigneth." (Revelation 19:6, KJV)

The multitude thunders. Heaven is not silent.

The multitude is not only seen, it is heard. It speaks, it sings, it thunders. And for those who resist God, this voice signals judgment. It is the roar of divine justice confronting the seductive and oppressive powers of the world. But for those who turn to God, that same voice brings comfort and assurance.

In Revelation 1:17–18, Jesus speaks directly to John: ***"Do not be afraid. I am the First and the Last, the Living One who died, but I am now alive forever and ever, and I hold the keys of death and Hades."*** And in Revelation 21:4, He adds: ***"He will wipe every tear from their eyes. There will be no more death or mourning or crying or pain, for the old order of things has passed away."***

These words are not whispered into isolation. They are framed by the LORD, echoed by the Angelic order, declared in the presence of countless witnesses. The great multitude is not just background, it is part of the message. It says: *This word is not empty. This promise is upheld by Heaven.* Whenever the Bible speaks of Angels as a multitude, it does so to add weight to God's comfort, strength to His promise, and immediacy to His presence. The Hosts appear not only to fight, but to encourage and affirm.

The prophet Daniel saw the same truth. In his own time of persecution and national disgrace, he too was granted a vision of the Host: **"A fiery stream issued and came forth from before him: thousand thousands ministered unto him, and ten thousand times ten thousand stood before him: the judgment was set, and the books were opened."** (Daniel 7:10, KJV)

In the face of uncertainty, Daniel was shown what John would later confirm: God is not outnumbered. His Hosts are beyond defeat. They are ready, willing, and positioned to serve.

The biblical concept of the multitude, especially in reference to Angels, is given for one great purpose: to bring comfort, encouragement, and assurance to those who receive the vision. It is not merely grandeur. It is divine nearness revealed through Heaven's numbers.

The Assurance of the Multitude

John's proclamation in Revelation 5:11 opens with a vision that still stirs awe: ***"And I beheld, and I heard the voice of many Angels round about the throne and the beasts and the elders: and the number of them was ten thousand times ten thousand, and thousands of thousands."*** (Revelation 5:11, KJV)

This is more than an image of scale. It is a declaration of reality, a multitude of Angels encircling the throne, worshiping the Lamb, and awaiting God's command. For John, and for the early Christians who first heard or read his testimony, this vision brought more than theology. It brought comfort, in the midst of persecution, hardship, and violent resistance to their faith.

Their suffering was real. But this multitude was a reminder: their pain was not a reflection of God's weakness or absence. When the moment comes for God to act and alter the course of history, His heavenly Host will not be lacking. No force on Earth or Hell can match His army.

Hell has numbers. Heaven has no limit.

John later expands this vision with even greater intensity: ***"And I heard as it were the voice of a great multitude, and as the voice of many waters, and as the voice of***

The Number of A Multitude

mighty thunderings, saying, Alleluia: for the Lord God omnipotent reigneth." (Revelation 19:6, KJV)

Here again, the sound is immense, a heavenly roar of praise. The multitude now includes not only Angels but redeemed humanity, all united in worship. They do not appear as a remnant, or a lucky few. They appear as a vast, victorious community, celebrating the fulfillment of God's justice and reign.

This is not a gathering of survivors. It is the unveiling of a people and a Host fulfilling the purpose for which they were made, to worship, to serve, and to reign with Him. What began in trial now ends in triumph. The multitude is not just the present they are forever active, fulfilling their design both in Heaven and beyond.

The multitude sings: trials end in triumph.

This vision reminds us that the future belongs not to the scattered or the silenced, but to the gathered worshipers of God, joined by the Angelic Host in everlasting victory. The worship in Revelation is not symbolic, it is a sign of settled reality: good has overcome evil, and those who have placed their trust in the Lord are not alone and never will be.

Those who believe in God are not few. They are not outnumbered. God possesses a vast and majestic army, already working to defend, protect, and carry out His will. Their presence is not just a vision for the end, it is a present assurance that His purposes will be fulfilled.

Elisha and the Eyes of Faith

Among the prophets, Elisha stands out as a man who did not merely believe in God's presence, he perceived it. His strength came not from natural advantage but from supernatural awareness. He knew something the fearful often forget: that the reality of Heaven does not disappear just because it is unseen.

One day, surrounded by a hostile army, Elisha's servant trembled in panic. But Elisha responded with unshakable calm: **"Fear not: for they that be with us are more than they that be with them."** (2 Kings 6:16, KJV)

Then he prayed, **"LORD, I pray thee, open his eyes, that he may see."** And the servant saw, not a wish or vision, but a mountain full of horses and chariots of fire, already surrounding them (2 Kings 6:17 KJV).

The Angelic multitude had not arrived in response to Elisha's prayer. They were already there. What changed was the eyesight of the

Faith doesn't create the Host- it reveals it.

servant. What changed was faith's ability to perceive what fear had hidden.

This is what God wants for all His people. Elisha's posture is not reserved for prophets, it is an invitation to every believer. To walk by faith is not to ignore earthly threats, but to be grounded in a greater awareness: that the battle is never ours alone, and that Heaven's army is never absent. We are meant to live with Eyes of Faith, eyes trained not only to believe in God's nearness, but to discern the activity of the multitude He has assigned to His people. These truths are not metaphor. The Host is real, present, and positioned for action.

The concept of the Angelic multitude is not a myth or a poetic tradition. It is revealed in Scripture as a factual spiritual system, designed by God, governed by His command, and dispatched for His people. We are not called to imagine them, we are called to trust in their presence and to partner with their readiness by faith.

This truth becomes especially vital in spiritual warfare. When conflict intensifies, when fear rises and pressure closes in, it is Eyes of Faith that determine our posture. Will we panic, or will we perceive? Will we freeze in despair, or will we stand, knowing that they who are with us are more than they who are with them?

The Gate of Number

A multitude signals more than numbers. It declares that God is:

- Sovereign – He has never been outnumbered. His Host surrounds us because He rules above all.

- Personal – He sends this Host not to decorate Heaven, but to protect His people and enforce His covenant on Earth.

- Loving – He made this multitude more than sufficient for every generation, every struggle, and every son or daughter who walks with Him.

And finally, this multitude anchors us in hope. The same Hosts who surround us in battle will one day gather in eternal worship. The vision of Revelation is not just a picture of Heaven, it is a promise to Earth: that those who walk with Eyes of Faith will one day see with perfect clarity what they once only perceived.

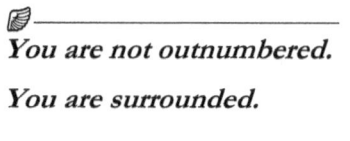
You are not outnumbered.
You are surrounded.

Let this assurance settle deeply:

- You are not alone.

- You are not uncovered.

The Number of A Multitude

- You are surrounded, by the presence of God and by His Angelic Host.

And when you believe it, the battle begins to shift.

The Great Multitude and the Eternal Family

The concept of the multitude extends far beyond the Angelic Host. It is also deeply connected to the community of the redeemed, those who have walked with God across time, now gathered into glory. Alongside the Angels, they form with all believers in Christ one eternal family, those in Heaven and on Earth united under the providence of the Creator.

This truth echoes throughout Scripture and shines clearly in the visions of the book of Revelation. The apostle John writes: ***"After this I beheld, and, lo, a great multitude, which no man could number, of all nations, and kindreds, and people, and tongues, stood before the throne, and before the Lamb, clothed with white robes, and palms in their hands."*** (Revelation 7:9, KJV)

This is a vision not of a few, but of a multitude no one could count, drawn from every human background and gathered before the throne in victorious worship. It is a picture of Heaven's inclusivity, of salvation offered without boundary, and of God's capacity to gather for Himself a people from every tribe and tongue.

John later records: ***"And I heard a great voice out of heaven saying, Behold, the tabernacle of God is with men… and God shall wipe away all tears from their eyes… neither shall there be any more pain: for the former things are passed away."*** (Revelation 21:3–4, KJV)

This multitude is not only victorious, they are eternally comforted. God dwells among them. He removes all pain. The former things are gone. The multitude is the community in whom God's redemptive purpose finds fulfillment.

> *Heaven's multitude doesn't just win-they are comforted forever.*

Hebrews echoes the same hope: ***"Seeing we also are compassed about with so great a cloud of witnesses… let us run with patience the race that is set before us, looking unto Jesus, the author and finisher of our faith…"*** (Hebrews 12:1–2, KJV)

These witnesses, those who have endured and remained faithful, surround us. Their presence is not just symbolic. It is a call to courage. Their testimony is not past, it is present encouragement, urging us forward with the assurance that we do not run alone.

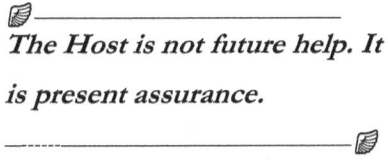

The Host is not future help. It is present assurance.

This vision of the great multitude would have brought profound hope to John and the persecuted Christians to whom he wrote. Many faced poverty, imprisonment, and death. And yet John shows them that the story does not end there. There is a multitude who have overcome, and they now worship in victory.

The multitude is a symbol of God's sovereignty, His faithfulness to all nations, and His triumph over evil. It demonstrates that salvation is not narrow in scope. It is vast, global, and inclusive, a redemption not for a few, but for a number too great to count.

This multitude is also a reminder of unity. Nations, tribes, and languages do not divide God's people. What unites them is not origin, but worship, love for God, faith in Christ, and membership in His eternal family. They are one people under one God, and nothing on earth or in hell can separate them from His love.

Importantly, this revelation often came in moments of fear or uncertainty. In Daniel's time, in Israel's conflicts during the books of Kings, and again in the churches of Revelation, the people of God faced enemies who seemed stronger and more numerous. But again and again, God gave them a counter-vision: a multitude that could not be overcome.

This multitude is still growing. Every day, believers who finish their race are gathered into it. Each one who belongs to Christ becomes part of this great community, not of limited number, but of endless increase.

This truth brings strength for today and hope for tomorrow. It reminds us that whether in joy or in suffering, we are never alone. We are part of something eternal, unshakable, and full of promise.

We are surrounded enough, seen and unseen, to never be left to fail.

Surrounded by Thousands

, Heaven's company is not distant, it walks with us

Throughout this chapter, we have traced the scriptural revelation of the vast and organized Angelic Host, "thousands upon thousands," gathered in majesty, aligned in purpose, and always under God's sovereign command. From the stars that fill the heavens to the multitude that surrounds His throne,

Angels don't symbolize-they serve.

The Number of A Multitude

every biblical image reminds us: God is never outnumbered, and neither are His people.

Just as He calls the stars by name, so too does He know and assign each Angel (Psalm 147:4). Their existence is not vague or symbolic; it is intentional, personal, and deeply aligned with God's care for His creation. In this, we find more than awe, we find assurance. For if He commands the Host, we are truly never alone.

This multitude is not merely a reflection of God's greatness; it is a living testimony of His readiness to provide, protect, and support. The Angels are not absent bystanders but heavenly responders, positioned to minister to those who belong to Him (Hebrews 1:14). In seasons of fear, isolation, or uncertainty, we can draw strength from the knowledge that God has surrounded us with an army, not to impress, but to intervene.

And this truth is not reserved for theological reflection. It is meant to be practical, present, and transformational. As we move forward in the chapters ahead, we will explore how this revelation becomes a part of our daily walk with God, not as abstract doctrine, but as a lived source of peace, confidence, and direction.

Revelation about the Host is not poetic-it's practical.

The Gate of Number

Take a moment to reflect:

- Where in your life do you need to remember that you are not alone?

- How would your decisions change if you lived with the awareness that God's Host stands at attention, not far off, but near?

This is not just about comfort. It is about empowerment. The Host that surrounds you is part of God's ongoing plan, not only for your protection, but for His mission on the earth. In the next chapter, we will begin to explore how this spiritual reality can shape your faith, infuse your prayers, and lead you to walk with greater boldness and clarity, knowing you are never disconnected from Heaven's purposes.

You are not just part of a local church or a moment in time.

You are part of a divine plan, backed by a divine army, guided by a divine King.

Chapter 3
To Meditate Further

1. How does the vastness of the Angelic Host shift my view of what's possible in my calling?

2. Have I underestimated the scale of Heaven's involvement in God's mission?

3. Where do I need to replace fear with the assurance of Angelic partnership?

4. How can I teach others about the nearness and readiness of the Host without mystifying or trivializing them?

5. What habits will help me stay spiritually aligned with Heaven's overwhelming support?

(2 Kings 6:16–17; Revelation 5:11; Genesis 28:12; Psalm 91:11–12; Matthew 26:53; Daniel 7:10; Luke 2:13–14)

IV

Singular Multiplexity

The Lord came from Sinai... with myriads of holy ones; at His right hand were flaming fire. **Deuteronomy 33:2**¶

The nature and organization of the Heavenly Hosts-emphasizes a plurality that is complex. This chapter explore how the deliberate choice of Jesus terminology hints at a deeper reality of the creativity of God. The chapter survey some taxonomies that reveal both the communal harmony and the unique roles within the angelic hierarchy. It observes however, the fact that our understanding remains limited. Angels straddle the boundary between the spiritual and physical realms, and our human language struggles to encapsulate their full reality. This calls for humility, recognizing that our comprehension is but a glimpse of the celestial symphony orchestrated by God. ¶

CHAPTER 4

SINGULAR MULTIPLEXITY

UNDERSTANDING MULTIPLEXITY

The pattern of Heaven is not simplicity, but unity in complexity

As we arrive at this final chapter of Part 1, we stand on a foundation already laid by the previous revelations. We have seen that we are surrounded by a great multitude, that the Hosts of Heaven are vast, intentional, and gloriously aligned. We have been reminded that we are not alone, and that both individually and as communities of believers, we are caught up in something far greater than ourselves.

But here, the insight deepens. What God reveals through the Hosts is not just that they are many, but that they are intricately diverse, each one shaped with unique roles, forms, and functions, yet flowing from a single divine Source. This brings us into the mystery of singular multiplexity, a heavenly principle that lifts our understanding even further.

Multiplexity does not mean disorder. It means structured complexity, a unity that does not flatten difference but orchestrates it. In Heaven, Angels are not identical. They are coordinated, not cloned. Their uniqueness does not threaten order, it fulfills it. They are bound by one allegiance but expressed through manifold forms.

This is the shape of Heaven's wisdom. The Hosts operate in obedience to one will, but they do so through many expressions. Their forms differ, their functions vary, their assignments are unique, but their allegiance is singular, and their movement is harmonized. In Heaven, diversity is not a threat to unity; it is the evidence of its depth.

> **Diversity is not Heaven's weakness-it is Heaven's signature of unity.**

Such a pattern is not foreign to Scripture. In the divine mind, one is never merely one. One Word creates many worlds. One God, three Persons. One Spirit gives many gifts. One Lord sends many messengers. One Kingdom, countless missions. Over and over, the Kingdom of God displays a harmony in which difference is coordinated, not erased. The Hosts of Heaven are a living reflection of this wisdom, each different, but none detached.

This insight into the Hosts opens a wider window: the logic of Heaven is multiplexity. And this logic is not limited to the celestial, it is invitational. It is to be called into it. The

Church on Earth, and every believer within it, is called to mirror this heavenly order: one body, many members; one Lord, many callings; one Spirit, many operations. It is invited to mirror their order, to walk in that same tension of unity and diversity, of harmony without uniformity.

Singular multiplexity is not a contradiction. It is the language of God's Kingdom, the structure of His purposes, and the logic of His communion. Heaven reveals not that complexity should be feared, but that complexity is sacred, when governed by the hand of God.

Understanding this prepares us for something greater than admiration. It prepares us for alignment. Heaven's unity is not static or mechanical. It is dynamic, alive, and purposeful. The Hosts show us the pattern. The Spirit invites us into it. The Hosts do not compete. They collaborate. They do not dissolve into sameness, they flourish in orchestrated complexity. And when we begin to see through this lens, we discover that Heaven's complexity is not a barrier, it is a doorway.

> **Heaven's unity isn't about erasing difference-it's about orchestrating it.**

To understand multiplexity is to see not confusion, but clarity. It is to recognize that God's wisdom builds through layers, not reductions. And it is to hear, perhaps for the first time, a deeper invitation:

Not just to observe Heaven's pattern,

but to join it.

Angels: A Diverse Types of Pluralities

, Not just many, but many in many ways

When we speak of the multiplicity of Angels, we are not referring only to their number. The Hosts of Heaven are not simply numerous; they are intrinsically diverse. They embody a plurality that is not accidental but intentional, not generic but particularized in form, nature, and assignment.

Each Angel reflects a distinct expression of divine intention. Though they share a common allegiance and origin, their identities are not uniform. Their features, their roles, their movements, even their appearances, a diversity so intricate that it calls us to wonder. No two are exactly alike, and none are unnecessary.

This is what we mean when we speak of multiplexity. It is not only that Angels are many, but also that they are many in many ways. Their plurality is layered. Their complexity is not a barrier to unity, but a revelation of it.

> *Layered plurality doesn't break unity-it reveals it.*

The Gate of Number

Over the centuries, both biblical interpretation and theological tradition have attempted to describe this diversity. Pseudo-Dionysius classification is the most famous. His initial sphere is composed of Angels that are the nearest to God and reflect His magnificence and sanctity. It is made up of Seraphim, Cherubim, and Thrones. (Isaiah 6:2-3; Revelation 4:8; Ezekiel 1:10,15-21; 10:14 1; Genesis 3:24; Exodus 25:18-22; 1 Kings 6:23-28; Isaiah 24:23; Revelation 4:4; 11:16; Ezekiel 1:15-21). Angels in the second sphere govern the universe and conduct God's will. The Angels recorded in that sphere are Dominions, Virtues, and Powers. (Colossians 1:16; Ephesians 1:21; 3:10; Ephesians 1:21; 3:10). The third sphere consists of the Angels who interact with human beings and the material world. It is constituted of Principalities and Archangels (Ephesians 1:21; 3:10; Colossians 1:16). Others have grouped them according to attributes, functions, or relational spheres. These efforts offer valuable glimpses, yet they also reveal how vast the mystery truly is. For every framework we attempt, there remains more hidden than explained. Angels defy neat categorization, not because they are chaotic, but because they are crafted according to the vast imagination of God.

Some thinkers have described Angels as personalized intelligences, or even as incarnate divine ideas, living symbols who not only serve but reveal dimensions of the Creator's will. Their very diversity teaches. It points us to a God who creates not by duplication, but by expression, a God who delights in variation as a language of glory.

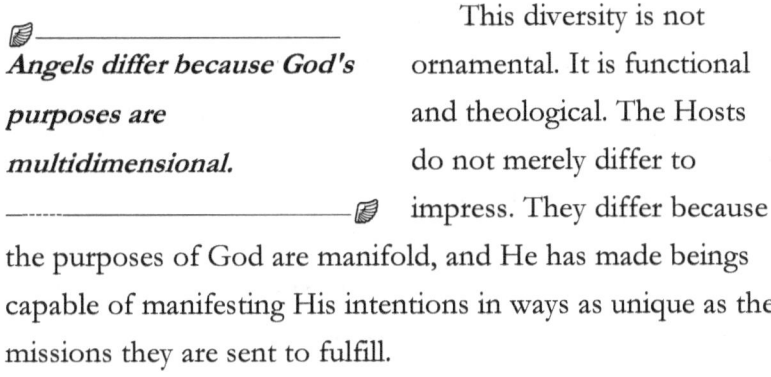
Angels differ because God's purposes are multidimensional.

This diversity is not ornamental. It is functional and theological. The Hosts do not merely differ to impress. They differ because the purposes of God are manifold, and He has made beings capable of manifesting His intentions in ways as unique as the missions they are sent to fulfill.

To behold the Host rightly, then, is to see divine complexity revealed in unity, not a chaos of spiritual beings, but a chorus of individualized ones, arranged not by sameness but by significance.

And this is not merely a celestial reality to be admired. It is a spiritual invitation. The Church, too, is called to learn from this diversity, to discern in it the nature of God, and to mirror its structure with reverence and faith.

Beyond the spheres of Angelic organization

The traditional model of the "nine choirs" or "orders" of Angels, seraphim, cherubim, thrones, dominions, virtues, powers, principalities, archangels, and angels, has long shaped Christian imagination. It provided an architecture of

The Gate of Number

reverence, a scaffold to glimpse the layered majesty of the Hosts.

Yet even the most elegant of these systems remains incomplete. These frameworks, while offering insight, are earthbound attempts to name what is, by nature, heavenly. They remind us that the diversity of the Angelic Host exceeds human comprehension. What is revealed to us is meaningful, but it is not exhaustive.

> *What God reveals is enough for trust-even if not for total knowing.*

In more recent biblical scholarship, some theologians have made the efforts to rearticulate relevant taxonomies that were left underdeveloped. One example is the work of Michael Heiser, who organizes Angelic beings into three theological "buckets":

- Nature (what kind of being they are)
- Status (their authority or location in the spiritual hierarchy)
- Function (their role or assignment)

This approach avoids flattening complex realities into a single hierarchy. Instead, it reflects a logic more consistent with the biblical witness: that identity, authority, and function often intertwine, but are not always interchangeable. An

Singular Multiplexity

Angel's role may shift. Its title may change depending on context. But its existence always flows from God's purpose.

Scripture confirms this fluidity. Angels are described by many titles: *sons of God, watchers, holy ones, spirits, stars, winds.* These are not just metaphors. Each name reflects something about their identity, mission, or realm of operation. To study their titles is to begin to glimpse the richness of Heaven's vocabulary, and the richness of God's imagination.

But the surprise of Scripture is not only in the classification of Angels, it is in how some of their titles are transferred to God's redeemed people. In the Old Testament, "sons of God" referred to celestial beings. In the New Testament, that same phrase is used to describe those who believe in Christ (John 1:12; Romans 8:14). The language shifts, not to erase the Angelic Host, but to signal a coming unity between the Heavenly and the earthly.

This is the direction of God's plan: ***"That in the dispensation of the fullness of times He might gather together in one all things in Christ, both which are in Heaven, and which are on earth."*** (Ephesians 1:10, KJV)

God is not creating two disconnected realms. He is drawing together a unified family, one in Heaven, one on Earth, brought into alignment under the headship of Christ. The Hosts and the redeemed are not strangers. They are members of the same divine household, each fulfilling roles that reflect the complexity and unity of God's Kingdom.

Heaven's Angels and Earth's redeemed belong to one family.

So to explore the categories of Angels is not a detour into mysticism. It is an invitation into alignment. The Church is not called to copy Heaven, but to partner with it, to learn its logic, its structure, and its collaborative movement under divine authority. In doing so, we come to see that every name and every role matters, not just in the heavens, but also in us. For the order of the Host is not merely a vision to admire. It is a template we are called to reflect.

This insight prepares us to explore something even deeper: not only are the Hosts themselves marked by complexity, but so too is the realm in which they dwell and operate. To understand the Hosts rightly, we must now look to the structure of the heavenly realms, for the order of Heaven is embedded not just in its messengers, but in its very fabric.

Heavenly Hosts and Heavenly Realms

, The complexity of Heaven extends beyond its messengers to its very structure

As we've seen, the Angelic Host is not only vast, but richly diverse, marked by distinct roles, titles, and configurations. But the Hosts do not float in abstraction. They operate within a complex spiritual environment, a realm that reflects the same multiplexity we observe in them. To grasp their purpose, we must understand where they operate. For just as the Hosts are not simple, neither is the space they inhabit.

Scripture does not describe Heaven as a singular, undifferentiated place. It speaks of "heavens" in the plural, even of a "third heaven" (2 Corinthians 12:2) and the "heaven of heavens" (Deuteronomy 10:14). These are not poetic flourishes. They are indicators of layered spiritual realities, realms that interact with one another and with Earth. Heaven, as revealed in the Word, is structured, dimensional, and active.

The Apostle Paul gives this mystery its clearest theological framing. In his letter to the Ephesians, he refers multiple times to "the heavenly places", not as static locales, but as dynamic arenas where blessing is bestowed, authority is exercised, and warfare unfolds (Ephesians 1:3; 2:6; 6:12).

The Gate of Number

It is in these layered realms that the Hosts of Heaven are stationed and sent. They do not operate in generality. They are

> *Angels don't drift-they're deployed.*

positioned strategically and relationally, within the invisible systems that govern the seen world. These heavenly places are more than stages, they are operational zones, in which Angels execute the will of God and contend with opposing powers.

And within this reality, we find both tension and comfort. On one hand, the spiritual realm is the arena of ongoing conflict. Forces of light and darkness contend. Realms are contested. Assignments are resisted. But on the other hand, these very heavens are the place where Christ now reigns.

"Far above all rule and authority and power and dominion… He sat down at the right hand of God in the heavenly realms." (Ephesians 1:20–21)

In Him, we too are seated, already positioned, though still on Earth, in a space of spiritual authority and communion (Ephesians 2:6). The complexity of the heavens is not foreign to us. It is the atmosphere in which we are called to walk and wage spiritual war (Ephesians 6:12).

> *God does not flatten reality. He layers it with wisdom.*

All of this reveals something essential about the mind of God: He governs through layered systems, not flattened control. Heaven's architecture is a living witness to His wisdom. It holds together realms of praise, judgment, intercession, warfare, and communion, all interwoven, all purposeful, all filled with Angelic presence.

And if even Heaven is structured in multiplicity, then we should not be surprised when God invites us to navigate complexity with reverence rather than fear. For what comes next is crucial: to walk with Heaven is not to claim mastery of these realms, but to recognize our need for help, for vision beyond our natural sight.

It is to admit what Elisha's servant had to learn: that even when we cannot see, there is more happening than we know.

BEYOND WHAT HUMANS CAN KNOW

, Faith begins where comprehension bows

As we begin to grasp the layered complexity of the heavenly realms, a necessary realization emerges: we have reached the limits of what human reason can apprehend. The Hosts are complex. The realms are many. The structure is

The Gate of Number

majestic. But we do not stand above it. We approach it as seekers, not as surveyors.

Jesus, in His teachings, repeatedly alluded to these celestial complexities, but not always through direct explanation. Instead, He spoke in a way that pushed the listener back to the Scriptures, where truths of Heaven are hidden like treasure. He invited pursuit, not presumption. His words became doorways into mystery, urging us to seek more, to wonder more, and above all, to trust more.

This journey of discovery, though beautiful, is not without challenge. We are creatures of sense and time, yet we are asked to perceive what is beyond both. The heavenly realm is not defined by what is visible or measurable. It moves to principles not accessible through touch or sight. And even when Scripture speaks of it, it does so through ancient languages and cultural codes, many of which remain difficult to translate or interpret.

Heavenly realities often involve social structures, ranks, and functions that have no direct analogy in the human world. While scholars have made great strides in decoding ancient texts and cultural patterns, the truth remains: some meanings elude us. Some words conceal more than they reveal. And some mysteries are not there to be solved, but to be honored.

These barriers are not failures. They are reminders. We were never meant to understand the things of God through intellect alone.

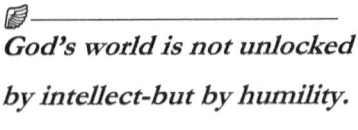

God's world is not unlocked by intellect-but by humility.

The deepest truths are revealed to the humble, not the proud, to those who approach not with control, but with dependence.

In fact, it is only when we reach the edges of our understanding that we become truly open to help beyond ourselves. The incomprehensible becomes approachable not through mastery, but through surrender. Mystery does not block us, it beckons us. And those who accept this will find that mystery is not a wall; it is a window into something greater.

This is why Scripture insists that divine knowledge comes by faith and revelation.

"For we know in part, and we prophesy in part… but when that which is perfect is come, then that which is in part shall be done away." (1 Corinthians 13:9–10)

The Gate of Number

Even Jesus' consistent use of the plural when speaking of Angels reinforces this reality. He did not present a simplified vision of the spiritual world. He unveiled its multiplexity, a world filled with beings whose roles, natures, and assignments intertwine far beyond human comprehension. It was a subtle way of saying: *you are part of something enormous, and it will not all fit in your hands.*

You don't have to hold it all. You just have to trust the One who does.

And that is the point. To walk with Heaven, we must bow before its mystery. Not to worship what we don't understand, but to worship the One who holds it all together. For it is in that posture of faith, humility, and openness that true revelation begins to flow.

MULTIPLEXITY IS PART OF THE UNIVERSE

, Creation reveals the mind of God in layered wonder

What we have seen in the Hosts of Heaven and in the layered structure of the heavenly realms is not an isolated spiritual pattern, it is a principle woven through all creation. The universe, from the subatomic to the galactic, speaks the same language: multiplexity is God's design.

Singular Multiplexity

The stars that stretch across space in countless formations, the intricate biology of life on Earth, the diversity of ecosystems and planetary systems, all these reflect a divine imagination that is not satisfied with simplicity. Like the Angelic Host, creation is filled with order and variety, with form and function, each element positioned with intentional uniqueness, each operating within a greater whole.

From starfields to seraphim, God designs with purpose and pattern.

This shared pattern between the heavens and the cosmos points to God's sovereign authorship over all realms. Both the seen and the unseen are His handiwork. Both reflect His boundless creativity and His precise order. Whether spiritual or material, all things function according to laws He has established. They are not in competition. They are echoes of the same wisdom.

And humanity, made in God's image, cannot help but feel drawn into this revelation. We are wired with a desire to know, to explore, to understand. Scientific inquiry, spiritual reflection, and divine revelation, these are not opposing forces. They are different responses to the same invitation: to behold the beauty of God's mind at work.

Creation is not random. It is not chaotic. It is a living revelation, designed to awaken reverence. The vast complexity of the universe and the Heavenly Host alike call

The Gate of Number

us to recognize the fingerprints of a skillful, relational Creator. Just as the Angels transcend the material and serve the purposes of God, the universe whispers of the transcendent. It beckons us to lift our eyes and ask deeper questions.

God's wisdom is evident in both the visible and the invisible. The spiritual realm, though beyond our senses, operates with divine precision. And the natural world, even in all its visibility, still hides a depth of order that humbles human understanding. In both realms, we are reminded that our task is not to conquer mystery, but to respond with faith.

We are not called to solve everything. We are called to trust the One in whom all things hold together.

"For we walk by faith, not by sight." (2 Corinthians 5:7)

In a world saturated with mystery, humility is not optional, it is essential. And for those who may be skeptical or indifferent, the invitation still stands. The sheer intricacy of creation challenges the idea of a meaningless universe. It suggests, with quiet insistence, that you are known, that behind the complexity is a relational God, who made you with purpose, and who understands your uniqueness more fully than you ever will.

To accept the complexity of creation is to begin the journey toward accepting ourselves as part of that design.

Singular Multiplexity

You are not a mistake. You are part of a system whose beauty is intentional. And God, who created such wonder, also invites you into fulfillment through relationship with Him.

This realization leads us to something deeply practical. What we observe in Heaven and in creation is not just for contemplation. It is a template for participation. The Church on Earth is called to reflect the same reality: diverse members in unified service. We will return to this theme in Chapter 8, where we explore how humility allows believers to honor each other's uniqueness while remaining aligned in purpose.

Like the Hosts, we are not meant to erase our differences, but to synchronize them in service. Through humility, we become collaborators with the divine. Through reverence, we begin to see complexity not as a problem to solve, but as a glory to walk in.

The God Who Knows Complexities

All of this, the complexity of the Heavenly Hosts, the layered structure of the spiritual realms, the intricate design of creation, leads us to one undeniable truth: God knows it all. Nothing about this divine complexity is accidental or out of control. Every function, every layer, every movement is held together by a God whose wisdom is not only infinite, but deeply personal.

The Gate of Number

Even as we marvel at the grandeur of the heavens, we are reminded that the One who created them is also the One who governs them. The vastness of the Angelic realms does not dilute God's nearness, it reveals His ability to be fully present in all things. He does not merely understand complexity. He designed it, He manages it, and He calls us to trust Him within it.

> *God doesn't just manage complexity-He designed it, and He walks us through it.*

As we wait for fuller understanding, the path forward is not through analysis alone, it is through faith. Revelation comes to those who walk humbly. We will never fully grasp all of Heaven's patterns, but we are not asked to. We are invited to trust the One who does. Mystery is not a failure of knowledge, it is a gift that calls us to deeper dependence on the Holy Spirit and deeper confidence in the goodness of God.

And in this, something remarkable emerges: If God pays such detailed attention to each Angel, if He assigns them individually, crafts them specifically, and entrusts them with unique missions, how much more does He care for you?

> *You are not lost in the layers. You are known within them.*

You, too, are known in your complexity. You are seen in your uniqueness. The layers of your personality, the contours of your voice, the shape of your mind, your

Singular Multiplexity

senses, body, temperament, gifts, and human connections, none of these are accidental. They are the raw materials of a life crafted for purpose.

The same God who assigns Angels to heavenly functions has created you with intentional design. You are not random. You are an irreplaceable part of His plan. And just as the Hosts serve with joyful precision, so too are you called to live with purpose, confident that God can orchestrate your life for His glory.

Jesus Himself affirmed this. His deep familiarity with Angels, expressed even in how He speaks of them, points to His authority over the heavenly realm. The One who knows the Hosts perfectly also reigns above them, and moves them on behalf of those He loves. His authority is not cold and distant. It is active, personal, and aimed at your redemption.

This is why you can trust Him. You don't need to understand every movement of Heaven to walk in its help. What matters is that He understands, and He invites you to collaborate, even when your vision is incomplete.

So ask yourself:

- Am I walking with the humility that Heaven models?

- Can I trust God's goodness even when I don't understand His complexity?

The Gate of Number

- Am I willing to welcome the presence and partnership of the Angels, even when I cannot explain all their ways?

Take time to pray. Ask God to awaken in you a posture of faithful participation, not fearful hesitation. Ask Him to help you move confidently into what He is doing, trusting that though you may not see the whole picture, He does, and the Angels He commands are working in ways that serve your calling.

Because this is not just about understanding Angels, it's about walking with them.

Not to control, but to collaborate.

Not to explain, but to fulfill.

Not alone, but as part of God's great commission in the Earth.

EMBRACING THE COMPLEXITY OF DIVINE DESIGN

, Harmony is not found in sameness, but in Spirit-led collaboration

As we come to the close of this chapter, and with it, the first movement of this book, we are left with a profound truth: God's design is complex, and yet utterly intentional.

Singular Multiplexity

From the Hosts of Heaven to the structures of the universe, from the inner workings of the Church to the soul of the individual believer, singular multiplexity is the divine pattern. Unity is never uniformity. In Heaven, harmony is built through difference, not despite it.

The Angelic Host stands as a living model. They serve one purpose under God's command, but each fulfills that purpose through distinct roles, forms, and functions. They do not compete. They do not envy. Each one, secure in its design, contributes with excellence. Diversity strengthens their unity, it does not threaten it.

> **In Heaven's logic, diversity is not a problem-it's power.**

This same pattern has been written into the Church. Every believer is a unique composition of history, personality, calling, and grace. We are not interchangeable parts. We are individually crafted instruments, each bearing a piece of the larger sound God intends to release through His people.

And yet, this diversity often feels overwhelming. In the messiness of human experience, across cultures, generations, and traditions, our differences can provoke comparison or conflict. But Heaven teaches us something different. It tells us that the multiplexity of the Kingdom is not a flaw to overcome, it is a strength to embrace. It is not something to solve, but something to steward.

The Gate of Number

This revelation demands a response. And the only response worthy of it is humility.

We are not called to understand every layer of God's design. We are called to trust it. We are not called to erase difference. We are called to honor it, to live in a posture of reverence, knowing that our part matters, but it is not the whole. That others' gifts matter, and so does the harmony we build together.

Humility doesn't shrink in complexity-it finds beauty in it. Humility allows us to see complexity not as chaos, but as beauty. It frees us from comparison, envy, and self-importance. It enables us to serve like the Angels, faithfully, joyfully, and in our God-given place, no more and no less.

This is not merely theological. It is deeply practical.

The Church cannot fulfill her calling if she only seeks sameness. We must become a people who create environments where uniqueness is welcomed, where spiritual diversity is not suppressed but channeled into shared mission. This is how we mirror the Angelic Host. This is how we prepare the Earth for Heaven's rule.

So now the question is yours to carry:

- Will you embrace your distinct role in God's design?

- Will you celebrate the differences around you, trusting that each part enhances the whole?

- Will you let go of comparison, and serve like the Angels, content, confident, and aligned?

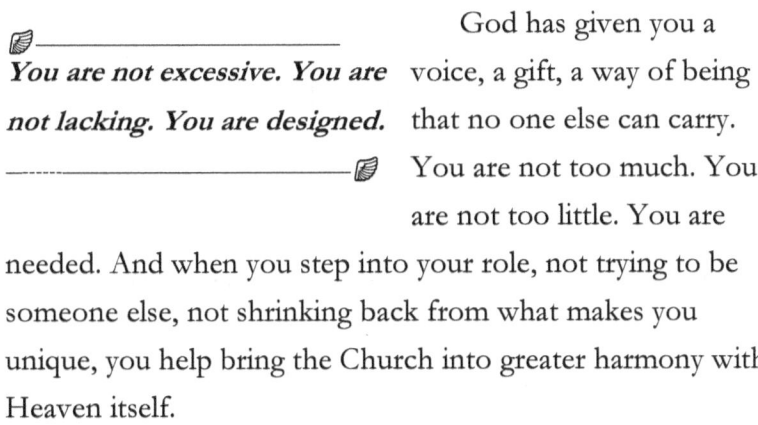

You are not excessive. You are not lacking. You are designed.

God has given you a voice, a gift, a way of being that no one else can carry. You are not too much. You are not too little. You are needed. And when you step into your role, not trying to be someone else, not shrinking back from what makes you unique, you help bring the Church into greater harmony with Heaven itself.

Let this final truth settle in your spirit:

True unity is not found in sameness. It is found in the harmony of diverse lives, moving together in faith, under the command of One King.

This is the wisdom of the Hosts. This is the invitation of Heaven. And this is the path forward as we prepare, in the next part of this book, to step into the practical alignment that makes this revelation walkable, personally, communally, and for the fulfillment of the Great Commission.

The Gate of Number

Chapter 4
To Meditate Further

- Where in my life have, I equated unity with sameness—and how might that limit my view of God's design?

- Do I tend to resist **complexity** in myself, in others, or in the Church? What would it look like to honor God through diversity instead?

- How can I grow in humility, so I respond to divine mystery with faith rather than control?

- What part of Heaven's order do I see reflected in my own design—my personality, gifting, or calling?

- What would it mean for me to walk in "Spirit-led harmony" rather than striving for conformity—in my family, church, or mission?

(Genesis 28:12–13; Psalm 103:20–21; 1 Corinthians 12:4–6; 1 Corinthians 13:9–10; Ephesians 3:10)

Part II

PART II.

THE PATH TO THE NUMBER

WALKING THE EARTH IN STEP WITH HEAVEN

Around the world today, the Church faces the unprecedented question of its real impact. Churches close their doors, not only for lack of faith or resources, but often for lack of collaboration. Buildings raised through generations of prayer and sacrifice are sold or lost. Ministries are shuttered, not because God has withdrawn, but because believers have resisted walking together in the unity that attracts Heaven's help.

Too often, the Hosts of Heaven remain unengaged, not due to unwillingness, but because the spiritual conditions needed for their work are not honored on Earth.

> *Heaven does not hesitate. It waits for alignment.*

What is lost in these moments is not only legacy or property, it is opportunity. The opportunity to reflect the harmony of the Heavenly Hosts, to build a local environment that mirrors Heaven's order and draws Heaven's help. When unity breaks, the Host is grieved, not because they lack

Singular Multiplexity

power, but because their mission is to reflect God's glory in cooperation with His people.

Walking into the Practice of Heavenly Partnership

Part I invited us to behold a profound mystery, Jesus' purposeful use of the plural when speaking of the Heavenly Hosts. We stood before that door and saw the light that spills through its frame: light on reverence, representation, sheer number, and heavenly complexity. We uncovered glimpses into the ordered, numerical structure of the Angels and their crucial role in the unfolding story of God's Kingdom. These revelations opened our eyes to the intentional design of the Heavenly Hosts and the seriousness with which God includes them in His Kingdom on Earth.

In the Kingdom, revelation is not for display-it's for movement.

But these insights were never meant to remain in the realm of wonder alone. Revelation, in the Kingdom, is always meant to be walked.

We now turn to that walk.

The question before us is not only what the plural "Angels" reveals, but how to walk in its light. If Heaven has not withdrawn, and the Heavenly Hosts are still appointed to

The Gate of Number

serve the heirs of salvation (Hebrews 1:14), then how shall we live in response?

Part II is the path. It is where the spiritual truth of the first section becomes the lived experience of the believer. This is the movement from mystery to practice, where theology becomes formation and revelation becomes relationship. This next stretch of our journey is about cultivating a life aligned with the order of Heaven, so that interaction with the Heavenly Hosts becomes not only possible, but natural. It is about preparing ourselves for an interactive relationship with Angels that is not merely symbolic, but operational, supporting the fulfillment of our personal calling and the Great Commission.

JESUS AND THE ANGELIC LIFE

The model has always been Jesus.

From His conception to His ascension, Angels accompanied Him. They appeared in dreams. They strengthened Him in solitude. They rolled away the stone from His tomb. They announced, warned, comforted, and protected. They brought messages and offered divine support.

The Path to the Number

They were not an accessory to His ministry; they were part of its infrastructure, divinely assigned participants and visible signs of Heaven's involvement in Earth's redemption (Matthew 1:20–21; Luke 1:26–38; Matthew 4:11; Matthew 26:53; Luke 22:43). So the question is not whether Angels walk with us, but whether we walk in awareness of them, with openness to their help, and with lives shaped to welcome their ministry.

Angels were not decoration in Jesus' life. They were divine infrastructure.

Jesus demonstrated what a life in divine-human-Angelic communion looks like. And He made it available to us. *"Whoever claims to live in him must live as Jesus did."* (1 John 2:6)

When Jesus spoke of calling "twelve legions of Angels" to His defense (Matthew 26:53), He wasn't speaking in metaphor. He was revealing a reality: He knew He had help, and He chose the cross anyway. His knowledge of Angelic presence was not exceptional, it was instructive.

Jesus didn't flaunt Angelic presence-He modeled how to walk in it.

If Jesus knew their nearness and walked in their partnership, how much more should the Church today learn to do the same?

The Gate of Number

Angels Still Walk Among Us

Heaven still responds to those who are open. The testimonies of God's people reveal that Angels are not absent. They are still ministering.

A woman once described seeing a bright figure intervene to stop a car accident, only for the figure to vanish once the danger passed. A father in North Carolina watched his daughter narrowly escape a burning house, carried by what she called "a man in white light" who told her where to run. A missionary in South America reported being shielded from gunfire, only to learn that his attackers had seen "two soldiers" standing at his side, though no one else was with him.

These are not myths. These are echoes of biblical truth lived in modern time.

Modern encounters are not myth-they echo Scripture.

The Hosts still help, still appear, still shield and strengthen. But they often do so in environments where hearts are open and unity is pursued.

The Path to the Number

THE HOSTS STILL MOVE. THE CHURCH MUST RESPOND.

From Genesis to Revelation, from apostolic testimony to modern encounter, the Hosts of Heaven have played an active role in announcing, protecting, guiding, and executing the will of God. And that role has not ceased. What remains uncertain is not their presence, but our readiness. The issue is not in Heaven. The issue is on Earth.

The question isn't whether Angels are present-but whether we're prepared.

Too often, the Church has treated the reality of Angels as myth or metaphor. But when we neglect the structures of Heaven, we forfeit the help of Heaven. Around the world, communities of faith fail, not merely because of outside opposition, but because they lack the unity, humility, and alignment needed to draw Angelic help. Buildings close, ministries dissolve, legacies end, not always for lack of people, but for lack of spiritual coordination.

In these stories, we see a mirror of something larger: the cost of neglecting Heaven's pattern.

When we ignore Heaven's order, we forfeit Heaven's help.

The Gate of Number

A Call to Discernment and Accountability

This portion of our journey will focus on discernment: how to recognize the presence and work of Angels in our lives, how to respond appropriately, and how to grow into that communion.

We'll learn how the New Testament affirms this expectation:

> ***"Are they not all ministering spirits sent to serve those who will inherit salvation?" (Hebrews 1:14)***

There is an implied accountability here. If Angels are ministering, then we are expected to be receiving. If they are sent, then we must be prepared to perceive and collaborate. This collaboration is not optional for the Church. It is essential if we are to fulfill the Great Commission and walk in the full authority and capacity available to us through the risen Christ (Matthew 28:18–20).

Angels are sent. The Church must be ready to respond.

The Principle Beneath the Path

To walk with Angels, we must walk like Heaven.

The Path to the Number

There is a foundational principle that guides this part of our journey. It is the thread that connects each chapter to come, and it explains why collaboration with the Heavenly Host is not just possible, but necessary.

There are two sides to Angelic intervention on Earth:

- There is the divine side, established and guided by God.

- And there is the human side, which requires intentional collaboration.

That collaboration is our responsibility.

- To collaborate, we must first connect.

- To connect, we must attract.

- To attract, we must resemble.

- To resemble, we must imitate.

And when we imitate the Heavenly Host, we create an environment that welcomes their work, and God's will is done on Earth as in Heaven (Matthew 6:10).

Imitation births resemblance.
Resemblance attracts Heaven.

This is the path to the number.

The Gate of Number

It is not mystical in nature, but practical and spiritual. It is the pathway of alignment, of becoming like those we are called to walk with. Jesus modeled this perfectly. He lived in unity with Heaven, and the Angels walked with Him. The more we resemble Heaven's order, through humility, holiness, prayer, and unity, the more Heaven moves with us.

> **Heaven moves not where we strive-but where we align.**

Not because we earn help, but because we become aligned with the environment of the Hosts.

From Mystery to Walking

This next phase of our book will begin to chart the ways the believer, and the Church, can walk into alignment with the Heavenly Host.

We will explore how:

- Angelic ministry interacts with the Church's mission

- Believers can cultivate the humility and unity that welcome the Host

- Spiritual disciplines prepare the atmosphere for collaboration

- The call to community echoes the unity of Heaven

The Path to the Number

- The Great Commission will not be completed without divine-human-Angelic partnership

The purpose is not to chase experience but to cultivate alignment with Heaven's order.

A Word to the Individual Heart

This path is not reserved for leaders or mystics. It is for you. You may feel insignificant or underqualified. But Heaven has never been interested in human credentials. What Heaven looks for is alignment.

> *Heaven is not drawn to status. It is drawn to alignment.*

If you long for greater clarity in your calling, if you hunger for Heaven's help in the ordinary battles of life, if you wonder whether your prayers matter, then hear this:

The Hosts of Heaven were sent for you.

And the path to their help begins in your heart.

As you read on, take time to pray. Ask the Holy Spirit to make you sensitive to the movements of Heaven. And be ready, because what begins as revelation may soon become encounter.

The Gate of Number

The Hidden Link: Angels and How We Treat Each Other

As we walk this path, one surprising truth emerges: Angelic collaboration begins in how we treat other people. It's easy to imagine mystical experiences. But Jesus, in all His divine glory, called us back to something deeply human: ***"Whatever you did for one of the least of these brothers and sisters of mine, you did for me."*** (Matthew 25:40)

When we learn to honor others as Heaven honors them, especially those who seem insignificant, we begin to align with the values of the Heavenly Hosts. Their ministry is not about spectacle, but service.

> *Heaven does not perform. It serves.*

"Do not neglect to show hospitality to strangers, for by so doing some have entertained Angels without knowing it." (Hebrews 13:2)

What's Ahead

As we walk deeper into Part II, we will:

- Learn how to welcome the Hosts of Heaven
- Cultivate the disciplines that draw Angelic help

The Path to the Number

- Follow Jesus' life as a model of spiritual cooperation

- Reflect Heaven's unity through Church-wide harmony

- Embrace our call to co-labor in fulfilling the Great Commission

You will not just understand Angels. You will begin to walk in step with them.

>The Hosts are not fiction.

>They are not far.

>They are not passive.

>They are near.

>They are active.

And they are sent for such a time as this.

Let us walk the path.

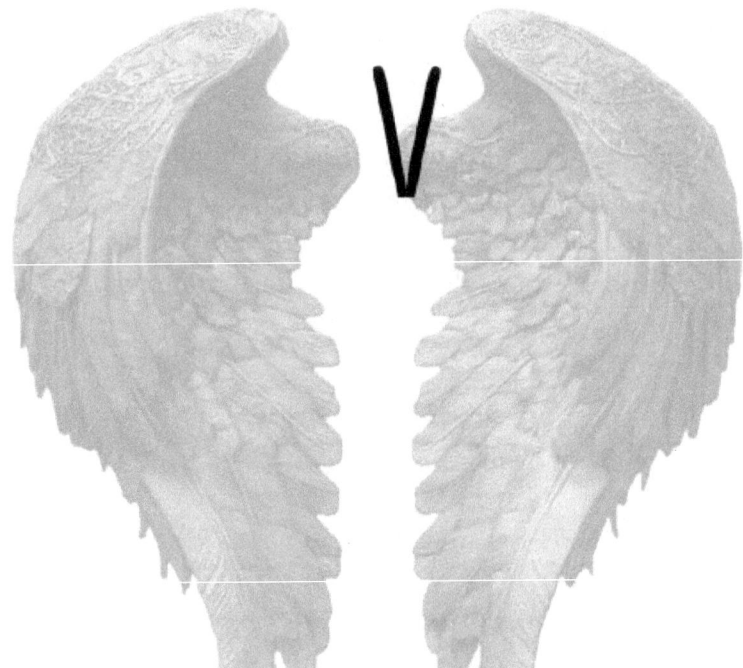

V
REVERENCE: THE POSTURE OF DESTINY

Take off your sandals, for the place where you are standing is holy ground. **Exodus 3:5**

Chapter 5 - Reverence: The Posture of Destiny opens Part II with a call to embody what Jesus revealed through His words and walk-a life aligned with the atmosphere of Heaven. This chapter moves beyond insight into application. It teaches how to live reverence in hidden spaces, daily routines, relationships, leadership, worship, and public engagement. Each sphere becomes a gate-either attracting or resisting Heaven's movement. Through practical reflections, the reader is equipped to cultivate environments where Angels feel at home and the Kingdom can advance.

The Gate of Number

CHAPTER 5

REVERENCE: THE POSTURE OF DESTINY

INTRODUCTION

In Chapter 1, we began our journey through the Gate of Number by observing Jesus' peculiar linguistic choice: His exclusive use of the plural form when referring to Angels. That choice was more than grammar, it was glory. It introduced us to a principle woven deeply into the structure of Heaven: reverence. Through His language, Jesus invited us to discern a divine decorum, one that acknowledged the majesty of the Heavenly Hosts and honored their place within God's order.

Now, in Chapter 5, we return to that insight, not merely to contemplate it, but to walk in it. What does it mean to live a life shaped by reverence? How can we move from insight to posture, from observation to transformation? This chapter builds a bridge between the theological truths we've discovered and the practical lives we are called to lead. Reverence is not merely a thought or an emotion, it is a posture, a way of walking through life with

> *Reverence is not a feeling. It is a way of walking.*

sacred attentiveness. It touches how we speak, how we work, how we relate to others, how we lead, and how we engage with the presence of Heaven around us. It also affects how we position ourselves to receive help from the Hosts of Heaven in order to fulfill our divine purpose.

Jesus, who modeled reverence in both word and conduct, gives us a path. And this path is not only for individuals, it is a call to communities, churches, and entire cultures to align with Heaven's tone. As we walk this chapter together, we will see that reverence is more than respect. It is a spiritual key. It opens environments to angelic activity. It signals readiness for divine collaboration. And it shapes the kind of people, and Church, through which Heaven is pleased to work.

Divine Help and Provision Are Available

We begin with a necessary and reassuring truth: divine help is available, and it is essential. For the revelations we have received so far in this journey are not mere insights to be admired, but truths to be lived. And living them, especially this posture of reverence, is not something we can do in human strength alone.

Reverence cannot be willed. It must be empowered.

The calling to walk in reverence, to cultivate an atmosphere that welcomes the Hosts of Heaven and

The Gate of Number

aligns with Heaven's decorum, demands more than good intentions. It requires divine empowerment. That is why God, in His mercy, makes provision. From the beginning, He has never called His people to a standard without also offering help to meet it.

> *Reverence aligns us with Heaven's rhythm and releases its help.*

Reverence is one such standard. It is not a feeling or fleeting emotion. It is a spiritual posture that shapes how we live in relation to God, to His works, and to all His creation, visible and invisible. It includes how we honor God Himself, how we treat people made in His image, how we respond to the presence of Angels, and even how we engage with creation's beauty, the unfolding of history, or a holy cause entrusted to us. Reverence is comprehensive. It touches everything. But here lies the challenge: our natural tendencies often lean toward casualness, self-centeredness, or forgetfulness of the sacred. And so, we need help. We need the Holy Spirit's renewing work in our hearts. We need the assistance of angelic hosts, dispatched by God, to accompany, align, and support us in cultivating the right atmosphere and fulfilling the call (Hebrews 1:14).

Jesus' use of the plural "Angels" was not just linguistically distinct; it reflected a heart attuned to the spiritual realm. That reverent awareness modeled the environment in which

Heaven's agents move. Reverence is Heaven's atmosphere. And when we live it, we align with divine rhythm, and unlock divine help.

Reverence Is a Gate

Reverence is not just a virtue, it is a gate. It is one of the thresholds through which we access the movements of Heaven. When reverence is present, something opens. Atmospheres shift. Invisible help becomes manifest. Angelic activity increases. Clarity of divine communication is heightened. And spiritual authority deepens.

Reverence draws God's gaze- and Heaven's response.

Scripture presents reverence as a disposition that draws God's nearness. "To this one I will look," says the Lord, "to him who is humble and contrite in spirit, and who trembles at My word" (Isaiah 66:2). Here we find a profound principle: reverence attracts divine attention. It prepares the environment for God's gaze, and by extension, for Heaven's intervention.

But let us be clear, this reverence is not limited to solemn church services or moments of overt spiritual ecstasy. It is a way of life. It governs how we treat the Scriptures, how

Reverence lives with eyes open to the invisible.

we speak of Jesus, how we interact with the Body of Christ, how we respond to divine promptings, and how we regard the presence and ministry of Angels. To be reverent is to walk in awareness. It is to recognize that we are never merely surrounded by the visible. **Reverence reminds us that even in the ordinary, the extraordinary may be waiting.** In this way, reverence becomes a gate, a place of encounter between what is natural and what is divine.

And where there is alignment, there is access.

The Environment of the Host

If reverence is a gate, then it also becomes an environment. It is not only a point of entry but a climate in which the Hosts of Heaven dwell and operate. Angels are shaped by what they behold. Day and night, they stand in the radiance of God's holiness. Their natural habitat is one of worship, awe, and perfect order. This means that when they are dispatched to Earth, they are drawn to places that resonate with the tone of their Home. Reverence, then, is not only a gate, it is spiritual oxygen. It creates resonance between our world and theirs.

> *Reverence is not optional-it is the atmosphere of Heaven.*

When reverence marks our homes, our prayers, our conversations, and our decisions, it creates a frequency to

Reverence: The Posture of Destiny

which the Hosts of Heaven respond. They find rest, not resistance. They find readiness, not noise.

Where reverence is cultivated, divine partnership is possible.

IRREVERENCE AND THE GRIEVING OF THE HOST

If reverence welcomes Heaven, irreverence sends it away.

Angels are not indifferent to our posture. They do not dwell where the sacred is mocked or treated as common. They withdraw from environments that clash with the holiness they carry. When we resist the tone of Heaven, through dishonor, carelessness, pride, or mockery, we grieve not only the Spirit (Ephesians 4:30) but the messengers He sends.

Heaven's Hosts do not stay where reverence is ignored.

Irreverence does not need to shout to be damaging. It can manifest in neglecting holy rhythms, dismissing godly counsel, or casually treating what God calls holy. These small cracks become wide gates of loss. Let us not grieve the Hosts God desires to send. Let us become once again the kind of people among whom Heaven is pleased to dwell.

Casual cracks open gates of divine retreat.

The Gate of Number

Jesus, the Model of Reverence

To understand reverence, we look to Jesus. His life was the embodiment of holy attentiveness. He moved in perfect agreement with the Father, speaking only what He heard, doing only what He saw (John 5:19). He handled Scripture with awe. He referenced Angels with intentionality. He addressed the Father with trembling love. And even in moments of great power, His tone remained aligned with Heaven.

Jesus did not teach reverence, He revealed it.

And if the sinless Son of God chose to walk in this posture, how much more should we? To follow Him is to imitate Him. And in imitating Him, we open our lives to the same spiritual partnership He modeled.

Walking It Out in Every Sphere of Life

Reverence is not meant to remain private. It is meant to be shared. What begins in one heart can spread to shape households, churches, cities. A culture of reverence becomes a landing strip for the activity of Heaven.

In such a culture, worship becomes offering. Scripture becomes encounter. Fellowship becomes sacred trust. Leaders become servants. Angels are recognized collaborators, not decorations in our theology. Let us not

Reverence: The Posture of Destiny

settle for occasional reverence. Let us build cultures that carry it daily. A culture where reverence dwells is one where Heaven moves freely.

Reverence is not seasonal inspiration, it is the spiritual tone of a life aligned with Heaven. It is a lifelong posture. And like any posture, it must be practiced, inwardly and outwardly, privately and publicly, personally and communally. It is one of the primary ways we mirror Heaven's culture on Earth, and one of the clearest signals we can send to the Hosts of Heaven: "This life is in alignment."

Below are six key spheres of daily life where reverence must be intentionally cultivated, not as performance, but as partnership with God's purposes.

1. Personal Spiritual Life: Reverence in Hidden Places

Reverence begins where no one sees. It forms in the way you treat the presence of God in your prayer time, your handling of Scripture,

> *Reverence is born in the unseen, long before it shapes the visible.*

your inner conversations, your responses to conviction. It is revealed in the quiet of dawn and the stillness before sleep.

The Gate of Number

- **Wake with worship**: Before engaging the world, engage the One who holds it. Whisper His name. Welcome His presence.

- **Handle the Word as sacred**: Open your Bible as if Heaven is speaking, because it is.

- **Receive correction with humility**: Reverence welcomes refinement. Let repentance be your friend.

- **Speak the Lord's name with care**: Let every mention of His name bear the weight of glory, not as filler, but as fire.

Heaven responds where hearts tremble rightly. The angelic Host moves toward those who take the Holy seriously.

2. Everyday Life and Work: Reverence in Routine

Reverence is not confined to the "spiritual" parts of your schedule. It reshapes how you carry your tasks, treat your space, and walk through your ordinary. Angels don't just visit altars, they walk through kitchens, offices, roads, and hospitals.

- **Do your work as worship** (Colossians 3:23): Offer every task, big or small, as unto the Lord.

- **Set apart moments for silence**: Even amid busyness, a pause can reset the atmosphere.

- **Treat material things with care**: The way we steward resources reflects reverence for the Giver.

- **Avoid careless words and shortcuts**: Speak and act with integrity, even when no one is watching.

The sacred is not just on the mountain, it is in the mundane. Reverence dignifies your daily.

3. Relationships with Others: Reverence in Human Connection

Every person you meet bears the image of God. Reverence honors that image. It governs how we speak, how we listen, how we confront, how we bless. Whether in family, friendship, ministry, or conflict, reverence brings Heaven's tone into human interaction.

To honor others is to recognize Heaven's imprint in human form.

- **Speak with intentional honor**: Avoid sarcasm, flattery, or speech that tears down. Bless instead.

The Gate of Number

- **Practice presence**: Look people in the eye. Listen as though their words carry weight.

- **Guard covenant relationships**: Marriage, friendship, mentorship, treat them as holy trusts.

- **Avoid familiarity with sacred roles**: Don't treat spiritual leaders or co-laborers as common. Walk in gratitude and honor.

Where there is honor, Heaven feels at home. Reverence humanizes and sanctifies our connections.

4. Leadership and Influence: Reverence in Responsibility

Leadership without reverence becomes manipulation. Influence without reverence becomes performance. Whether you lead a prayer group, a business, a classroom, or a nation, reverence anchors your authority in the fear of the Lord.

Authority without reverence is no longer leadership-it becomes control.

- **Lead with the weight of eternity in view**: Every decision echoes beyond the moment.

- **Model what you preach**: Reverence is contagious, but only when it is authentic.

- **Seek Heaven's tone, not just outcomes**: Don't sacrifice the sacred for success.

- **Honor those you lead**: Shepherds walk among sheep with dignity and care, not control.

Where reverence shapes leadership, the angelic can partner without obstruction. Such spaces are safe for divine assignment.

5. Community and Church Life: Reverence in Worship and Fellowship

A community without reverence is a club. A church without reverence is a stage. But when reverence marks a gathering, Heaven joins it.

> *Without reverence, gatherings become performances-not places of presence.*

The Hosts of Heaven are drawn to holy unity, to awe-filled worship, to spaces where the presence of God is not assumed but adored.

- **Approach worship with expectancy**: Enter His courts with thanksgiving, not entertainment (Psalm 100:4).

- **Protect sacred rhythms**: Make time for prayer, fasting, communion, and shared repentance.

The Gate of Number

- **Uphold order and spiritual covering**: Spiritual protocol is not control, it is alignment.

- **Value the presence, not the platform**: Celebrate His nearness more than human personalities.

The early Church grew in power because it walked in awe (Acts 2:43). The same is true today.

6. Social and Cultural Engagement: Reverence in the Public Square

Our reverence must not disappear when we enter the arena of media, politics, or advocacy. If reverence is real, it will shape how we address injustice, how we use our influence, and how we speak into the culture. We are not only representatives of truth, we are representatives of tone.

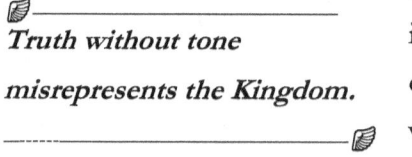
Truth without tone misrepresents the Kingdom.

- **Engage the world with dignity**: Let your public voice carry Heaven's character, not just reaction.

- **Honor even when you disagree**: Do not curse what God still desires to redeem.

- Speak of Angels, demons, and spiritual realities with sobriety: Don't trivialize the sacred for effect.

- **Live as a signpost**: Let your lifestyle reflect the holiness of God in secular spaces.

The Great Commission is not a casual assignment. It requires reverent ambassadors who embody the message they carry.

Final Invitation: Reverence as a Way of Life

This is how we begin to live what we have seen. Not in bursts of inspiration, but in the slow, deliberate shaping of atmosphere and action. Reverence becomes the gate we walk through daily. And it becomes the gate through which angelic help flows, divine purpose unfolds, and the Kingdom advances.

And because they walk in reverence, they move in power, toward the fulfillment of the Commission for which Heaven stands ready to assist. Let it be said of us: *"These are they who walk with God's tone. These are they among whom Heaven rests. "*

Chapter 5
To Meditate Further

- How can I practice reverence in the unseen and ordinary parts of my day?

- What does it mean for me to walk reverently in leadership, and how do I guard against manipulation?

- How can my community (church, family, team) grow in reverence together?

- What would change in my worship or service if I saw Angels as present and participating?

- In the public sphere, how can I represent the tone of Heaven, not just the truth of Heaven?

(Exodus 3:5; Colossians 3:23; Ephesians 4:30; Micah 6:8; Hebrews 12:28; Ecclesiastes 5:1; 2 Timothy 2:24–25.)

VI

Unity: The Posture OF Partnership With Heaven

"How good and pleasant it is when God's people live together in unity… for there the Lord bestows His blessing." **Psalm 133:1–3**

Unity: The Posture of Parnership with Heaven

Chapter 6 - Unity: The Posture of Partnership with Heaven reveals that unity is not simply a human ideal-it is a Heavenly reality. This chapter invites the reader to walk in that same posture. Drawing from the patterns of the Host, the chapter outlines seven principles of Heavenly unity and offers practical steps for cultivating it in every area of life. In doing so, it fulfills the goal of this part of the book: helping believers align their lives with Heaven's way so they can partner more fully with its mission. Unity, rightly practiced, becomes a force that attracts Angelic movement and sustains spiritual momentum. Without it, we cannot carry Heaven's purpose with power.

Unity: The Posture of Parnership with Heaven

CHAPTER 6

UNITY: THE POSTURE OF PARTNERSHIP WITH HEAVEN

INTRODUCTION

In Chapter 2, we uncovered spiritual insights surrounding the concept of collective representation. We explored how Jesus' distinctive way of referring to Angels revealed powerful truths about their unity. We saw how Angels, as part of a well-jointed body, work together with shared identity and purpose. They embody a heavenly model of collaboration under God's authority, a model established and upheld by God Himself. This collective identity is not only a defining characteristic of Angels; it is also meant to serve as a divine blueprint for how the Church should function in its mission on earth. Just as Angels fulfill God's will with shared purpose and identity, the Church is invited to live in unity as part of God's larger plan.

In this chapter, we shift from theological reflection to practical application. The power of togetherness, whether in worship, prayer, or service, is key to unlocking the full spiritual potential of the Church. When believers gather

> *When purpose unites us, Heaven joins us.*

with a shared purpose, they open the door to deeper collaboration, not only with one another but also with the angelic realm, working in partnership to accomplish God's will on earth.

This chapter provides concrete steps to foster unity and cultivate collective action within the Church and in the personal spiritual lives of believers. Readers will learn how to develop an interactive relationship with Angels, align with their heavenly purpose, and empower their church communities to function in harmony, mirroring the divine cooperation we examined in Chapter 2. Through these practical applications, the believer begins to experience the full spiritual potential God intends for His Church as we move toward collaboration with both the heavenly and earthly saints.

We will explore how believers can build this interactive relationship with Angels, aligning their spiritual efforts with divine order. This includes recognizing the angelic role in empowering our spiritual journey and understanding the ways Heaven and Earth are designed to function in unified action.

Finally, we'll examine how unity and collective action, both among fellow believers and with the angelic realm, enable the Church to fulfill its destiny in advancing God's Kingdom. Unity is not merely a lofty ideal; it is a vital, practical tool for empowering the Church to accomplish God's purposes on earth. Throughout this chapter, readers

Unity: The Posture of Parnership with Heaven

will find biblical examples, practical steps, and spiritual reflections to help apply these insights to everyday life. As believers engage these principles, they will find their personal faith strengthened and the unity of the Church deepened, working together to unlock the transformative power of unity and divine collaboration.

But before we move further, let us return to the events surrounding the passion of our Lord Jesus. There we find both a foundation and a light that guide us into the practice of unity we are about to explore.

A Reflection of Trinity

In the final hours before the crucifixion, Jesus prayed. He prayed for His disciples, for those who would believe after them, and for the Church throughout the ages. This was not just any prayer, it was the last great intercession before His sacrifice. And in that sacred moment, His heart turned toward one primary concern: **unity**.

His words in John 17 are full of tenderness and urgency. Jesus knew the challenges His followers would face persecution, distraction, division, and the subtle drift into individualism. He knew the spiritual battle that would surround the birth and growth of His Church. And so, He prayed: *"that they may be one, as We are one"* (John 17:21).

> *Disunity doesn't just divide-it distorts Christ's witness.*

This was not a theoretical or symbolic prayer. It was deeply strategic. Jesus understood that the success of the Church's mission would depend on its unity. He said that the world would believe in Him through the visible oneness of His followers. That means disunity does more than damage relationships, it misrepresents Christ to the world.

But His prayer also reached beyond human relationships. Jesus was pointing toward a unity that reflected something eternal, the very unity of the Trinity. The Father, Son, and Spirit are distinct but never divided. They move in perfect communion, mutual honor, and shared purpose. Jesus wanted His Church to operate from that same place of divine harmony.

This is not only a model for human community; it is a **gateway into cosmic collaboration**. The unity of the Trinity forms the foundation for all heavenly unity, including the unified movement of the angelic Host. Angels operate in perfect order and alignment because they reflect the nature of the God they serve. They are many, but they move as one.

Jesus' prayer, then, was not only about interpersonal unity within the Church. It was an invitation into **divine

> *Unity is not just about us-it's alignment with Heaven.*

Unity: The Posture of Parnership with Heaven

alignment, a unity that spans Heaven and Earth. To respond to this invitation is to embrace a lifestyle of partnership with God's nature, God's people, and God's messengers.

The unity Jesus longed for is both relational and functional. It is the kind of unity that allows Heaven to cooperate with Earth. When believers live in that kind of harmony, they create an atmosphere that welcomes the angelic host and advances the Kingdom of God.

This is the unity that Angels recognize. It is the unity that mirrors the Trinity. And it is the unity that Jesus still prays for today.

UNIQUE PRINCIPLES OF HEAVENLY UNITY

The model of the Heavenly Hosts' unified structure is marked by several unique principles that the Church can emulate to enhance its organization, its effectiveness, and its alignment with the actions of the Heavenly Hosts. These principles offer a guiding framework for cultivating a strong, unified, and purpose-driven community. They are not revolutionary concepts, and it is not surprising that many churches or networks of churches have, in one way or another, attempted to implement them.

What must be intentionally added, however, is a critical reflection on how these principles align with Heaven's order

The Gate of Number

and how they relate to our Heavenly ministry Helpers. That reflection opens the door for a more effective spiritual partnership.

The First Principle:

Establish a structured leadership that reflects what is in Heaven.

This principle has historically taken on different forms, each with its justifications. But what would a local church look like if it became more aware of Heaven's model and embraced an intentional desire to collaborate with the Heavenly Hosts more effectively?

The Church must continue to grow in its understanding and teaching of the importance of clear, biblically qualified leadership structures. These should follow the pattern of the Heavenly model. The application of this principle includes more than the administrative functions of elders and pastors who provide spiritual direction and oversight (1 Timothy 3:1–7; Titus 1:5).

Heaven honors order. The Church must embrace it too.

It must also include a growing awareness and development of the fivefold functional ministries set in place by the Lord. These ministries include the functions of Apostles, Prophets, Evangelists, Pastors, and Teachers. These are the very gifts that Christ received and distributed as a result of His victorious passion, His sacrifice for the edification of the saints and for the fulfillment of the ministry He entrusted to the Church.

The Second Principle:

Assign specific roles and responsibilities to various members, as it is done in Heaven.

To understand the Heavenly order, we must consider the socio-cultural setting in which the biblical descriptions of that order were first revealed. Such an understanding enables us to apply the foundational principle of contextual adaptation in an effective way. It allows the Church to follow the living direction of the Holy Spirit.

This principle, like the first and the ones that follow, requires the Church to persevere in developing ministry teams with clearly defined roles that address the wide range of needs within the Body (1 Corinthians 12:4–11). However, what is most urgent in this season is that both ministry teams and individual workers lift their eyes upward, to align their structure and conduct with that of the Heavenly Hosts who, as the Lord promised, labor with them every day (Matthew 19:29).

The Third Principle:

Foster spiritual unity, with a focus on being led by the Spirit.

The order among the Heavenly Hosts is maintained by a higher level of communication. They are led by the Spirit of God, not by routine consultations or committees. There is an invisible thread that connects them, flowing from the throne. The instructions they follow, even in large numbers, reflect a kind of unity that is anchored in reverence for God and in relational harmony with the other Angels.

Likewise, the Church should develop the ability to discern God's voice and follow His guidance as one people. This sensitivity to the Spirit requires maturity, unity, humility, and ongoing spiritual training.

Purpose is the gravitational force of Heaven's unity.

Unity is not just about agreeing on doctrine or direction; it's about walking in the Spirit together (Galatians 5:16, 25). When the Church is led by the Spirit and nurtures the fruit of the Spirit in its life together (Galatians 5:22–23), it mirrors the alignment of Heaven.

This kind of unity enables believers to respond quickly to divine promptings and to move together in one Spirit, without unnecessary friction. It fosters an environment where the angelic Host can move freely among God's people.

The Fourth Principle:

Establish systems of accountability and submission, reflecting the hierarchy and humility observed in Heaven.

Angels, despite their varied ranks and powerful capacities, are deeply aware of their need for order and accountability. Their effectiveness depends on this structure. They are not independent actors; they function under command, always in harmony with those who are above, beside, or under them. Their power is not in personal autonomy, but in corporate alignment and willing submission to divine authority.

The Church must recover this same value. The Body of Christ is not a collection of spiritual freelancers but a well-joined spiritual family and army. It must therefore uphold the twin virtues of honor and humility. Honor builds strength; humility preserves unity.

Heaven isn't run like a machine. It flows like a family.

This principle calls for members to walk in accountability, not out of fear, but out of a shared commitment to reflect the heavenly structure. It demands that leaders submit to God and to one another, that teams respect divine order, and that individuals value being part of something greater than themselves.

When this happens, the Church begins to reflect the spiritual posture of the angelic Host. Angels are not drawn to pride or chaos, but to environments that look like Heaven, where order is honored, authority is submitted to, and all movement begins with humility before the King.

The Fifth Principle:

Foster a culture of prompt and coordinated obedience, mirroring the immediacy of angelic response in Heaven.

Angels do not procrastinate. Their responses to divine instruction are immediate. They move swiftly, without negotiation or hesitation, because their unity is bound to their responsiveness. Delay weakens unity; prompt obedience reinforces it.

In the same way, the Church is called to cultivate a culture where instructions from the Lord are not only discerned together, but acted upon together. When God speaks, whether through His Word, His Spirit, or His messengers, unity is expressed in the shared commitment to move as one.

Without unity, even the right direction becomes the wrong destination.

Such coordinated obedience does not suppress individuality; it channels it toward a common direction. Teams, ministries, and entire communities become more effective when they are trained to recognize and respond to the Spirit's timing in unity.

The Church must be ready to act, not just as individuals but as a synchronized body. When members hesitate or lag behind, momentum is lost. When they move together, Heaven draws near. Unity becomes visible, tangible, and powerful.

The Sixth Principle:

Promote reverence as a foundation for unity, just as it defines the atmosphere among the Heavenly Hosts.

In Heaven, reverence is not a suggestion, it is the atmosphere. Angels veil their faces before God, not because they are uncertain or afraid, but because they are deeply aware of His holiness. Their unity is shaped and sustained by this awareness. Every movement, every assignment, every proclamation is carried out in profound reverence for the One who sits on the throne.

The Church, too, must learn to walk in reverence, not only for God, but for His Word, His people, His call, and His ways. Reverence protects unity. It silences pride, tempers opinions, and curbs impulsiveness. Where reverence increases, alignment becomes easier. People listen better. They speak more carefully. They follow with more intention.

This principle calls for a spiritual posture that is attentive, humble, and worshipful. It invites the Church to approach its mission, its gatherings, and its relationships with a sense of sacred responsibility. When reverence is present, the Church

> *Heaven's Hosts respond where Heaven's culture reigns.*

becomes a place where Heaven feels at home, where Angels move freely because the atmosphere reflects their own.

The Seventh Principle:

Strengthen shared purpose as the binding force of unity, just as it is in Heaven.

In the Heavenly realm, unity is anchored in purpose. The angelic Host is not merely bound by shared space or identity, but by a clear, God-given mission. Every Angel serves the fulfillment of God's will. Their unity does not depend on emotional connection, it depends on alignment with divine purpose.

Heaven's center is not a preference. It is a Throne.

Likewise, the Church must ground its unity in a shared commitment to the will of God. Too often, disunity arises not because of personal offense, but because purpose has been lost or replaced by secondary priorities. When God's purpose is central, personal agendas fade. Vision becomes clear. Direction unites.

This principle urges churches and ministry teams to regularly return to the question: What are we here for? What has God called us to accomplish together? As that purpose is clarified and elevated, distractions lose their grip. Disagreements diminish in size. Unity becomes easier to sustain because it is bound by something greater than preference, it is tethered to God's eternal mission.

When purpose is strong, unity becomes durable. And where there is purpose-driven unity, the angelic Host stands ready to collaborate.

While these principles may seem lofty, they are not beyond reach. They are real, and they are meant to be lived. But living them requires more than agreement, it demands courage, humility, and a willingness to begin again. One pastor learned this the hard way.

When Church Walls Came Down

A pastor of a mid-sized congregation in Virginia told this true story originally published in Guideposts We don't know his name, but his story has been shared as a testimony of humility, failure, and the kind of unity that can only be built through repentance. In the early 2010s he faced a crisis he never anticipated. Here is what he shared.

'I used to believe that unity was something you could preach into existence. That if you just taught the right doctrine, and everyone had the same spiritual goals, harmony would follow. I was wrong.

Several years ago, I pastored a mid-sized congregation in the South. We were faithful, active in missions, and proud of our legacy. But under the surface, fractures had begun to form, divisions I didn't fully see until they erupted.

It started with a disagreement about leadership appointments and ministry priorities. One group wanted to lean into outreach; another felt we were neglecting the core congregation. What began as discussion turned to suspicion. Soon, people stopped talking to each other. Ministry teams split. I even heard rumors that some members were planning to leave and start a separate church.

As a pastor, I was devastated. I had taught about unity from the pulpit. I had cast vision and quoted John 17. But I hadn't realized that heavenly unity, real unity, requires more than shared information. It requires spiritual posture. It requires humility, obedience, reverence, service, faithfulness, and a life of regular prayer.

At first, I tried to fix things administratively. Meetings, emails, conflict resolution protocols. But none of it changed hearts.

One morning, in deep prayer, I felt the Spirit press me: You're preaching unity, but you're not walking in it. Lead with repentance, not authority.

So I did. I called a leadership meeting, not to defend my decisions, but to confess. I admitted where I had overlooked warning signs. Where I had favored strategy over spiritual sensitivity. Where I had spoken at people instead of listening to them. I asked for forgiveness.

To my surprise, others followed. People who hadn't spoken kindly to each other in months began to open up. Some cried. Others shared their own part in the division. We stayed late, prayed together, and something changed.

In the weeks that followed, our congregation began to heal. We restructured our ministries, not just around tasks, but around teams committed to serving one another. Worship deepened. Outreach became collaborative again. And most powerfully, there was a new sense of presence, as if Heaven had reentered the room.

Unity had not come easily. It required brokenness, surrender, and persistent prayer. It wasn't clean or quick. But it was holy. And it taught me this: the unity of Heaven only becomes real among us when we embrace the posture of Heaven.'

Unity: The Posture of Parnership with Heaven

> *Unity grows where space is made-not just where opinions match.*

This Pastor shared that the breakthrough hadn't come through strategy or planning. It came when he embraced the postures Heaven responds to: humility, obedience, reverence, faithfulness, and prayer. These were not leadership techniques. They were Kingdom postures.

His story reminds us that the principles of unity in Heaven are not easy to live on Earth. They demand more than agreement, they demand surrender. But where they are embraced, unity becomes more than a theory. It becomes a channel for divine power and angelic alignment.

And so, as we turn to the next section, *Unity Attitudes, Values, and Behaviors*, we do so with this in mind: the practices that support unity are not theoretical ideals. They are the soil in which Heaven plants supernatural fruit.

Unity Attitudes, Values, and Behaviors

In addition to the seven core principles of heavenly unity, we must adopt specific attitudes, values, and behaviors that allow us to practice and sustain that unity in everyday life. These inner postures align us with Heaven's ways and build the kind of spiritual atmosphere where the angelic Host can operate freely among us.

The Gate of Number

The list below does not claim to be exhaustive, but it offers practical pathways that allow Heaven's patterns to shape our human relationships and ministry partnerships. These are not personality traits, they are spiritual disciplines. Each one plays a role in making us a people who carry and protect unity as Heaven does.

Humility

Humility is not simply modesty, it is the recognition that we are part of something bigger than ourselves.

Heaven celebrates position without competition.

It is the attitude that enables us to take our place without striving for position or recognition. In the Heavenly Host, every Angel serves with full awareness of divine hierarchy and with no jealousy of another's role. In the same way, humility allows us to celebrate others, listen well, and lead without controlling.

To walk in humility is to continually defer to God's will, seek the good of others, and release pride. It is the soil in which all other attitudes grow.

"Do nothing out of selfish ambition or vain conceit. Rather, in humility value others above yourselves" (Philippians 2:3).

Obedience

Obedience is Heaven's language of trust. The angelic Host responds instantly to God's instructions. Their loyalty is not proven by emotion but by action. In the same way, our unity is strengthened when we respond quickly and faithfully to what God says, whether through Scripture, the Spirit, or spiritual leadership.

Heaven speaks trust through obedience.

Obedience helps eliminate confusion and discord. It keeps us moving together. It is also an act of worship, signaling our readiness to join Heaven's flow.

"If you love me, keep my commands" (John 14:15).

Reverence

Reverence is the posture of awe and honor. In Heaven, nothing is casual. The Angels cover their faces, proclaim God's holiness, and treat their assignments with sacred weight. Reverence on earth is not about formality; it is about remembering who we are and who we serve.

Reverence creates safety. It protects sacred things from being mishandled. And

Reverence guards what is holy and draws what is heavenly.

The Gate of Number

it fosters unity by helping us treat one another and our callings with honor.

"Therefore, since we are receiving a kingdom that cannot be shaken, let us be thankful, and so worship God acceptably with reverence and awe" (Hebrews 12:28).

Service

Service turns unity from principle into practice.

Service is the practical expression of unity. Angels minister. They serve not to gain status, but because that is their purpose. In the Church, unity grows when we show up to serve, not just to be served.

Service invites collaboration, breaks pride, and creates trust. It helps each person see their value in the Body and keeps us moving outward toward God's mission.

"Each of you should use whatever gift you have received to serve others, as faithful stewards of God's grace in its various forms" (1 Peter 4:10).

Faithfulness

Faithfulness is not just about longevity; it's about consistency in love and responsibility. The Hosts of Heaven are unwavering in their assignments. They are not driven by mood or moment, they are governed by loyalty to the King.

We reflect this when we remain steady in prayer, presence, and service, even when it is inconvenient or unnoticed. Faithfulness becomes a glue that holds people together and allows trust to deepen over time.

Without faithfulness, unity is only a moment.

"Now it is required that those who have been given a trust must prove faithful" (1 Corinthians 4:2).

Regular Worship and Prayer

Worship and prayer are Heaven's rhythms. In the throne room, Angels never cease to worship. They listen, respond, and align with the will of God in ongoing cycles of reverence and declaration.

When the Church prays and worships regularly, especially together, we recalibrate ourselves to God's voice and rejoin Heaven's cadence. Prayer and worship create space for alignment, healing, direction, and unity.

Unity is not built in silence. It is sustained in worship and prayer.

"Pray continually, give thanks in all

The Gate of Number

circumstances; for this is God's will for you in Christ Jesus" (1 Thessalonians 5:17–18).

These attitudes are not optional for those who seek unity, they are necessary. They cultivate a heart posture that not only aligns us with one another, but with Heaven itself. And when practiced regularly, they create an atmosphere where unity becomes sustainable, and supernatural help becomes normal.

We Are Not Isolate Champions

God does not work with isolate champions. His plan was never to raise up spiritual celebrities or solo performers. His desire has always been to build a Body, a people, a family, a company moving in unity with Him and with one another. From Genesis to Revelation, we see God working through collective identity and covenant community.

Isolation depletes. Unity sustains.

Heaven itself is structured this way. Angels do not work alone. They are part of a well-ordered Host, assigned, aligned, and in step with God's agenda. Their unity makes their movements powerful. Their coordination reflects Heaven's glory.

This is the pattern God has given to us.

Yet, too often in the Church, we reward isolation and celebrate independence. We admire those who "do it all" or "stand alone," and in doing so, we risk losing the very power that unity makes possible. The truth is that isolation is not a badge of strength, it's a barrier to divine cooperation.

God is raising up a generation who understands that unity is not weakness. It is the strength of Heaven. He is forming teams, networks, and communities of believers who are joined in vision, function, and spiritual rhythm. These are the people Heaven partners with. These are the movements Angels are drawn to.

To live this way, we must reject the mindset of spiritual isolation. We must embrace accountability, shared leadership, and mutual honor. We must learn to move together.

And when we do, we won't just have better relationships, we'll walk in greater power. We will function like the angelic Host: many, but one. Distinct, but united. Positioned, and moving together.

This is the posture of partnership with Heaven. It is the key to unlocking supernatural momentum. It is the way forward for the Church.

The Gate of Number

Chapter 6
To Meditate Further

- Do I see unity as a spiritual atmosphere that attracts Heaven, or merely as human agreement?

- Where am I resisting unity because I'm confusing it with sameness?

- In what areas of my life or ministry have I made function more important than relationship?

- Have I isolated myself under the banner of strength, rather than choosing partnership for lasting impact?

- How can my posture—tone, humility, and deference—help preserve unity in my church, team, or family?

(Psalm 133:1–3; 1 Corinthians 12:12; Amos 3:3; John 17:21; Colossians 1:18; Ecclesiastes 4:9–10; Ephesians 4:2–3)

Unity: The Posture of Parnership with Heaven

Assurance: Being A Part of Thousands

Do you think I cannot call on my Father, and He will at once put at my disposal more than twelve legions of Angels? **Matthew 26:53**

Chapter 7 - Assurance: Being Part of Thousands invites the reader to walk in the deep confidence Jesus implied when He spoke of "the Angels" in the plural. This chapter unpacks what it means to live with the awareness that we are part of a vast, divine multitude actively working in alignment with God's purpose. More than comfort, this truth provides courage, responsibility, and perspective. It shifts us from limited thinking-like the idea of one Guardian Angel-to the biblical vision of Heaven's coordinated Host. This chapter reminds us that divine assurance is not for passivity. It is for alignment. We move with Heaven when we believe we are surrounded by it. And when we live like those who belong, we step boldly into God's mission.

Assurance: Being a Part of Thousands

CHAPTER 7

ASSURANCE: BEING A PART OF THOUSANDS

LIVING IN THE ASSURANCE OF ANGELIC PRESENCE

In Chapter 3, we explored the profound truth of the overwhelming number of Angels surrounding the believer. Some versions of Scripture describe it as "ten thousand times ten thousand, and thousands of thousands." As we noted then, human language falls short when trying to articulate the scale of realities in the spiritual realm. The expressions used in Scripture do not quantify the Angelic Host; they highlight its vastness. This heavenly multitude is not only immense, it is divinely organized and intentional.

> *The Angels are not looking for heroes. They are looking for disciples.*

This understanding opens our hearts to a unique assurance. The countless Hosts of Heaven are not passive beings; they were created with purpose. Their presence in the divine order reveals not only the magnitude of God's power

The Gate of Number

and sovereignty but also His loving care for every individual. The believer is never truly alone, not in spiritual warfare, not in daily life, not in moments of calling or crisis. He is part of a vast spiritual family, actively supported by an organized and innumerable company of Heavenly Hosts.

> *You are never truly alone. Not in battle. Not in life. Not in calling.*

In this chapter, we will build upon the theological foundation laid in Chapter 3 and move into practical territory. The aim is to help believers not only acknowledge but internalize and activate this spiritual assurance in everyday life. It's about moving from truth into application, learning to walk, pray, serve, and lead in the confidence that Heaven's armies are with you. This confidence is not meant to inspire pride, but to deepen our faith and strengthen our walk of obedience. When we align with this divine reality, we position ourselves to live and minister with the power and peace that come from Heaven's design.

The Spiritual Reality of Being Part of God's Immense Household

Every believer is part of God's celestial family. This family is not simply symbolic or spiritual in the abstract, it is living, active, and vast beyond comprehension. It includes, by divine design, the multitude of Angels who make up what

Assurance: Being a Part of Thousands

Scripture calls the "Heavenly Host." These are not distant or detached beings. They are full members of God's Household, and their presence is integral to the experience and mission of the believer.

One of the defining traits of this family is its extraordinary number. The scale of Heaven's population is intentionally emphasized in Scripture, not to be calculated, but to be revered. The multitude is described in terms that stretch the boundaries of numerical comprehension: "ten thousand times ten thousand, and thousands of thousands" (Revelation 5:11; Daniel 7:10). These expressions are not poetic exaggerations; they are theological signals. They tell us that there is more than enough. The sheer number of Angels reflects God's intention to meet the full scope of His redemptive plan.

But this multitude is not a passive crowd. It is a functional force. Angels were created not as ornamental symbols but as achievers, fulfillers, and helpers of the divine purpose. They are not bystanders in the story of redemption, they are participants, actively working in service of God's will on the earth. Their presence reinforces a truth the Church must reclaim: Heaven is not far off, and it is not silent. It is at work.

God made this multitude on purpose. He created them to be sufficient, not just in number, but in capability, to accompany humanity in fulfilling His divine plan. They exist

The Gate of Number

to support God's purposes, to assist His people, and to magnify His glory. They move in response to His commands and align perfectly with His desire to see His Kingdom come on earth as it is in Heaven.

> **God doesn't rule alone. He commands an innumerable army.**

This is why Scripture so often identifies God as "the Lord of Hosts." He is the Commander of this innumerable army. This title is not ceremonial, it reveals the very nature of divine governance. God rules not alone, but with an organized and submitted multitude. The fact that He surrounds Himself with such a company should say something to us. It means He values order, teamwork, loyalty, and execution. It also means that what He sets in motion will not fail. His army does not rebel. His Host does not resist. His purposes are not abandoned midway. They are fulfilled with unity and precision.

For the believer, this is not just theological truth, it is spiritual assurance. It tells us that we are not part of a struggling or improvised mission. We belong to a Household that functions under the leadership of the Almighty Commander, supported by a Host that does not falter. This assurance should not remain theoretical. In the sections that follow, we will begin to explore how this truth translates into lived experience, how being a part of this multitude can shape our responses in the everyday realities of life.

From Theology to Application: Welcoming the Unseen Support into Every Domain of Life

As we move forward, we will explore what this assurance looks like in practice. While the truths we've shared so far are deeply spiritual, their relevance extends far beyond spiritual language. The presence and function of the Angelic Host intersect with every aspect of human experience. Whether psychological, emotional, social, or ministerial, the truth of our belonging to God's multitude has real consequences.

That said, what comes next may feel, at times, less overtly spiritual in its presentation. Some applications will sound technical. They will speak to the inner workings of human thought, behavior, and communal interaction. That is by design. Our goal is not to isolate the spiritual from the practical, but to show how they interweave.

If you are inclined to explore these bridges between theology and daily life, keep reading, you will discover how the Angelic Host relates to your internal battles, your calling, your atmosphere, your leadership, and your emotional resilience. If you are more drawn to the deeply spiritual dimensions, you may choose to move ahead to later sections where those themes are more prominent.

The Gate of Number

> *You belong to a family of many. The multitude of Heaven is your household.*

But no matter your preference, do not lose sight of this foundational truth: you are part of a family of many. That family includes the multitude of Heaven. And from that identity flows both your assurance and your authority.

There is Power in the Many

The familiar saying "safety in numbers" is not a random phrase, it captures a profound spiritual and psychological reality. Human beings are wired for belonging. We instinctively seek security in the company of others, and we draw strength from being part of a larger collective. This design is not an accident of evolution but a deliberate imprint of the Creator. God formed us to function in the context of community, and He reflected that same design in the invisible realm.

Being part of a multitude provides assurance. This assurance is psychological, social, and ultimately spiritual. Studies across various disciplines, from psychology to sociology and anthropology, confirm that people find greater emotional stability and courage when they know they are not alone. The realization that we are one among many often gives us the strength to persevere, to hope, and to act boldly.

This truth has direct application to the believer's understanding of the Angelic Host. Belonging to the multitude of God's family, which includes innumerable Angels, is not symbolic, it is a foundation for faith and confidence. The knowledge that we are part of something so vast and purposeful reshapes how we face life's challenges.

> *You are not part of a symbol.*
> *You are part of a strategy.*

Larger groups tend to possess greater resources. Tangibly, a large group can offer more protection, more shared wisdom, and more strength. Intangibly, it increases morale and confidence. Individuals within such a group feel less exposed and more empowered. This is true in military units, in communities, in prayer movements, and it is profoundly true in the Kingdom of God.

When believers understand that they are accompanied by a multitude, they no longer view themselves as isolated in their spiritual journey. The overwhelming scale of God's angelic army gives us more than a poetic picture, it offers assurance that there is more than enough divine help available to meet every need. This is not a fluctuating resource. Human numbers may rise and fall, but the numbers of the Heavenly Host are fixed and unfailing. Their strength does not weaken. Their loyalty does not waver. The assurance they provide never expires.

The Gate of Number

In social contexts, belonging also validates identity. When people are surrounded by others who share their purpose, they are less likely to feel alienated. The presence of others affirms their sense of direction and builds confidence in their decisions. This phenomenon, often called "social proof," means that when many people are committed to a cause, others are more likely to perceive that cause as worthy or true. In fact, the bandwagon effect, where belief and behavior gain momentum simply by being popular, further intensifies this cycle.

While such psychological validation can be beneficial, human collectives are not always reliable sources of truth. Some group identities, ideologies, or cultures may reinforce beliefs that are harmful or even destructive. This is why the assurance that comes from belonging to the multitude of Heaven is different. It is sound. It is safe. It is anchored in divine glory. The identity we receive from knowing we are surrounded by the Hosts of Heaven is a healthy one, it is rooted in the presence of God and leads to identification with Heaven, not with the trends of man.

In larger groups, shared beliefs and values tend to become more pronounced. There is less ambiguity and more direction. A clear mission creates unity, and unity creates assurance. This is especially evident when the group is mobilized for a defined purpose. As believers, we are part of a divinely defined cause, one that spans Heaven and Earth.

Our association with the multitude of God's family provides more than emotional comfort; it provides clarity of purpose and direction.

> *Assurance isn't to soothe you. It's to send you.*

Culturally, belonging to a large and recognized group is often equated with legitimacy. The more people affirm a belief, the more confident others feel in joining it. This cultural instinct is amplified in the digital age, where influence and numbers are visibly counted and celebrated. While this dynamic can sometimes be shallow, it does speak to an underlying truth: people feel safer when they are not alone.

Historically, large movements have often succeeded in shaping societies. Religions, reformations, and social movements have drawn power from their numbers. This reinforces the belief that size contributes to legitimacy. But again, the difference lies in the source. The power of the multitude we are speaking of is not sociological, it is divine.

Even today, this dynamic continues. Being part of a multitude still provides emotional and strategic security. When we share burdens across a group, individual fear is diminished. Responsibility becomes manageable. Risk feels less overwhelming. This is especially important in seasons of uncertainty, transition, or spiritual warfare. We draw strength from knowing others are standing with us, even if those others are not seen with the natural eye.

The Gate of Number

But the influence of a large group is not always positive. Peer pressure and the desire to conform can cause people to adopt harmful ideas just to fit in. Normative social influence, the tendency to conform in order to be accepted, can lead people down paths that do not align with truth or goodness. This is why discernment is essential.

While human collectives may lead astray, the multitude of Heaven never does. Its unity is not based on social convenience but on submission to the will of God. Jesus Himself consistently used the plural when speaking of Angels, not as a rhetorical flourish, but to point to a reality we must not ignore: Heaven is not sparse. It is populated. And that population surrounds us.

The presence of thousands upon thousands of Angels is not a metaphor. It is part of the assurance of God. We are not alone, not in the night, not in the crisis, not in ministry, not in temptation. We are part of a multitude that God Himself has appointed for our support.

This sense of assurance is not just helpful, it is vital. At times, the believer may feel isolated, abandoned, or overwhelmed. But such feelings are not the final truth. The truth is that no believer, no matter how hidden or wounded, is ever alone. The company of Heaven is ever-present, ever-willing, and ever-strong. The One who commands legions of Angels still commands them today. He commands them for His purposes, and for you.

Assurance: Being a Part of Thousands

Living with the Awareness of Divine and Angelic Presence

Some years ago, I read a minister's story about an unexpected encounter that left a lasting impression on him, and now, on me as well.

He had been out doing evangelism when he met a man who appeared friendly at first but carried an edge of defiance in his spirit. The man invited him to sit and talk. As they conversed, the topic quickly shifted to faith, temptation, and moral consistency.

Then came the challenge.

"Suppose I offered you a drink right now," the man said, holding up a bottle.

"And suppose there was no one around, no wife, no church members, no one to see or judge. Would you drink it with me?"

It was a classic test, the kind that probes for cracks in a person's convictions. The minister paused, not because he was tempted, but because he recognized the moment. Then he answered:

"You may not see anyone else here, but I am never alone."

The Gate of Number

There was silence. The man looked puzzled, maybe even a little convicted.

"God is with me," the minister continued, "not as a policeman watching to punish, but as a Father who loves and strengthens me. And more than that, His Angels are present. I may look alone to you, but I'm surrounded."

The statement wasn't for effect. It was the fruit of deep awareness, an internalized truth that the minister lived by. He had trained his heart to live in the presence of God, and in doing so, had also become deeply aware of the Heavenly Hosts that move with those who walk in obedience.

This kind of assurance doesn't come from mere head knowledge. It is cultivated through intimacy with God and attentiveness to the spiritual reality that surrounds the believer. And though it may not always be easy to explain, those who walk closely with God begin to sense it in very real ways, especially during moments of spiritual warfare, moral temptation, or difficult decisions. There is great strength in knowing you are not alone. When temptations arise, or fear creeps in, or compromise whispers its subtle invitation, the assurance of God's presence, and the presence of His Angels, becomes a powerful shield. We are never abandoned. Never forsaken. Never truly outnumbered.

That minister's words echo through this chapter: "I am never alone." They reflect a spiritual posture we're all invited to grow into, a posture rooted not in fear of being seen, but in joy at being surrounded.

From Guardian Angel Thinking to Multitude Awareness

The Bible speaks not of one Angel-but of multitudes in motion for God's people.

For many believers, the idea of angelic help is reduced to a single comforting thought: the presence of *a* guardian Angel. This notion, while not entirely unbiblical, is often shaped more by folklore and children's stories than by the full testimony of Scripture. The result is a faith that envisions divine support as minimal and fragile, a lone celestial figure quietly trailing behind us.

But that image falls short of the truth.

The Bible paints a far more expansive, majestic picture. The Hosts of Heaven are not a handful. They are a multitude, countless in number, arranged in ranks, and fully aligned with God's purposes. They are not background decorations to our faith journey. They are part of the divine infrastructure of Heaven's mission on Earth.

Elisha, the prophet, once found himself in a seemingly desperate situation. Surrounded by enemy forces, his servant panicked. But Elisha remained calm, not because he denied

The Gate of Number

the threat, but because he saw what others could not. He prayed, "Lord, open his eyes that he may see," and suddenly the servant's eyes were opened to a hidden reality: the hills full of horses and chariots of fire all around Elisha (2 Kings 6:17). The man of God did not just believe in one Angel, he believed in thousands upon thousands, positioned for protection and ready for action.

This was not new to Elisha. His predecessor, Elijah, had been taken up in a whirlwind, escorted by a heavenly entourage that included chariots and horses of fire (2 Kings 2:11–12). These were not poetic metaphors. They were revelations of actual beings, angels in ranks, moving with power and purpose.

Scripture does not suggest that Angels multiply. They are not born or reproduced. Their number is established, set by God and sufficient for every generation. They are many. They are enough. Yet despite this truth, many believers still operate with a "just one Angel" mentality. Their theology limits their expectation, and their expectation limits their experience. They do not walk in the awareness of Heaven's scale because they have never been invited to imagine it, and certainly do not believe for it.

Heaven's Hosts are not asleep. They are active, alert, and aligned.

Assurance: Being a Part of Thousands

But Heaven invites us to expand our faith. Jesus never said, "If you have the faith of a mountain..." He said, *"If you have faith as small as a mustard seed"* (Matthew 17:20; Luke 17:6). Even a small measure of faith can open access to the vast resources of the Kingdom. Faith is not about deserving, it is about receiving.

The Heavenly Host is not assigned based on our worthiness but aligned to God's purposes in us. When we believe what God has revealed, when we ask Him to open our eyes as Elisha did, we begin to see that we are not walking alone. We are accompanied, not by one invisible figure trailing behind us, but by an army moving in sync with God's call upon our lives. It is time to shift from the comfort of the individual guardian to the strength of the collective Host. The reality of angelic support is not fragile, it is overwhelming. It is not scarce, it is abundant. And the more our faith expands, the more our lives begin to align with the reality of Heaven's multitude.

ACCESSING THE ANGELIC SUPPORT ASSIGNED TO YOUR DESTINY

The assurance of angelic presence is more than comforting truth, it is a Kingdom invitation. But like many dimensions of Kingdom life, it operates on faith. God has assigned the Hosts of Heaven to serve His people, but they do not move by default. Their activity is often unlocked by our spiritual posture: our faith, our alignment, and our obedience.

Every believer is born with a divine assignment. No one comes into this world without a purpose rooted in God's design. And to every purpose, God assigns provision, including spiritual reinforcement through His Angels. These Angelic messengers and warriors are real. They are specific. They are available. But they must be activated.

THE PATHWAY OF FAITH.

Many people never experience the full help available to them simply because they never believe for it. Others believe in God generally but remain unaware of this dimension of divine support. Still others are vaguely aware, but have never received the kind of spiritual revelation that transforms awareness into expectation. And so, though Heaven's multitude stands ready, they often remain disengaged.

Jesus taught that faith as small as a mustard seed can move mountains (Matthew 17:20; Luke 17:6). This means that massive shifts can begin with the smallest spark of living faith. It also means that when faith is dormant or absent, movement stalls. Not because God is unwilling, but because Heaven's design honors and responds to believing hearts.

But this truth carries a sobering parallel.

Just as the Angels of the Lord are activated by faith and obedience, there are also spiritual powers aligned with darkness, what Scripture calls "principalities, powers, and rulers of darkness in this world" (Ephesians 6:12). These forces, often described as "angels of iniquity," are empowered by sin, idolatry, rebellion, and unbelief. As evil increases among men, the influence of these unholy forces expands. In many places, they have remained unchallenged, not because they are stronger than the Hosts of Heaven, but because faith has not risen to confront them.

This should awaken us.

The Angels of God's justice, holiness, healing, and intervention are ready. They await the obedience, the prayers, and the proclamations of those who walk in covenant with God. But they will not move without alignment. In the same way, the unchallenged ground continues to echo with the voices of other powers, not because the cross was insufficient, but because the authority it secured has not been exercised by the Church. To expand the reach of the Kingdom, we must expand the reach of our faith. To fulfill the Great Commission, we must move beyond symbolic agreement and into active spiritual engagement. Faith is not just for internal peace, it is for external mission. It activates Heaven's Host to push back darkness, enforce the victory of Christ, and accelerate the spread of the Gospel.

This is not fantasy. It is strategy. Kingdom strategy.

The Gate of Number

Faith is the key that unlocks angelic collaboration. Revelation feeds that faith. Obedience channels it. And love sustains it. Let us not die without having activated the help Heaven has made available. Let us not allow angels of iniquity to operate unopposed while the Angels of God remain assigned but unengaged. Let us become a people of active, mature faith, those who inherit promises, push back darkness, and live with the full assurance of angelic partnership.

You were born with purpose. You were born into a Kingdom. And that Kingdom has assigned you help.

Activate it, by faith.

Enjoying the Power of 'the Multitude'.

There is no motivation more compelling than the deep conviction that what we are pursuing is truly worth it, and that it is aligned with God's purpose. This is especially true when it comes to the revelation of angelic presence. The awareness that we are surrounded by a multitude of Heavenly Hosts should not remain a theological concept tucked away in spiritual reflection. It is meant to be lived, experienced, and enjoyed in everyday life.

The Host is not a theory to contemplate. It is a presence to live with.

In life's real battles, Heaven's help becomes real.

This multitude of Angels becomes particularly meaningful when we face real-life situations, when praying for protection, discerning direction, battling fear and anxiety, engaging in spiritual warfare, or carrying out specific ministry assignments. These are the very moments where the assurance of angelic collaboration can move from abstract knowledge to lived experience. In these situations, the presence of Heaven becomes tangible.

But this kind of spiritual confidence does not emerge automatically. It is something we grow into. The believer is invited to develop a confident and consistent application of this truth, not as a mystical curiosity or exaggerated fantasy, but as a grounded reality rooted in God's Word. As Scripture reminds us, *"faith comes by hearing, and hearing by the Word of God"* (Romans 10:17). We grow in assurance by anchoring ourselves in what God has spoken.

And yet, this journey is not just about comfort or empowerment. The unfolding of a relationship with the Hosts of Heaven also transforms the one who seeks it. Our character is refined, and our posture before God is shaped as we learn to partner with His unseen servants. This is part of the faith journey, a transforming faith that, over time, learns to recognize, honor, and live in sync with the multitude God has provided.

The Gate of Number

Personal Challenges and Crises

Remember: those who are with us are more than those who are with them. (2 Kings 6:16-17)

There are seasons in life when nothing around us seems to point toward victory. Circumstances can appear dark, confusing, or overwhelming. It is in these moments, when our natural senses are clouded and the way forward seems uncertain, that the awareness of angelic presence becomes a vital anchor for the soul.

The multitude may not change your storm-but it will change your stance.

When the believer embraces this truth, they begin to see challenges differently. The knowledge that thousands of Angels surround them does not instantly change external circumstances, but it transforms internal posture. Instead of responding in fear, anxiety, or despair, they can draw strength from the unseen reality that Heaven is actively involved.

In times of crisis, the multitude of Angels is not distant or passive. They are present and attentive, carrying out assignments from the throne of God. Though invisible, their presence brings tangible encouragement. The believer is not left alone to navigate hardship. Whether the difficulty is

Assurance: Being a Part of Thousands

emotional, relational, financial, or spiritual, they are upheld by a divine network of help.

As this awareness grows, it becomes more than comfort, it becomes strength. The believer learns to live with the assurance that even in trials, they are never forsaken. They stand not only in the promises of God but also among His servants, the Hosts of Heaven, who move with Him to accomplish His will. That reality offers not just reassurance, it imparts boldness.

You don't just stand on promises-you stand among Heaven's Hosts.

Spiritual Warfare

Remember: ten thousand times ten thousand are standing before GOD reading to exert HIS judgment (Daniel 7:10)

One of the most immediate and powerful ways to enjoy the reality of the multitude is in the context of spiritual warfare. Whether the battle is personal, communal, or missional, believers are not called to fight alone. The assurance that "ten thousand times ten thousand, and thousands of thousands" of Angels are present and active (Daniel 7:10) becomes a vital source of strength and courage.

Spiritual warfare is real. It may not always be visible, but it is constant. The believer faces opposition from spiritual forces that seek to resist the purposes of God. But we are not left defenseless. We are surrounded by a multitude that is not symbolic but functional, an army of Angels aligned with God's will and ready to respond to faith-filled action.

These Angels are not passive observers. They are participants in the ongoing conflict between the Kingdom of God and the forces of darkness. But their participation is not automatic. As with every dimension of the Kingdom, faith and revelation are the keys. The more space we make for their involvement, through faith, proclamation, and alignment with God's Word, the more present and active they become in our battles.

Daniel 7:10 gives us a vivid glimpse into this spiritual reality: "A fiery stream issued and came forth from before Him: thousand thousands ministered unto Him, and ten thousand times ten thousand stood before Him: the judgment was set, and the books were opened." This is not distant imagery, it is a picture of divine order, Angelic readiness, and judicial authority moving into action at the throne of God.

Spiritual warfare isn't begging- it's alignment with the Host.

When we internalize this truth, it should reshape how we pray. Spiritual warfare becomes less about pleading and more about partnering. We are not begging for help; we are aligning with Heaven's army. Our words matter, not because they manipulate God,

Assurance: Being a Part of Thousands

but because they reflect agreement with His Word and His ways.

This is why **declaration** and **request** are both essential.

- **Declaration** builds faith. It establishes our awareness and affirms truth in the atmosphere.

- **Request** calls upon God to act according to His revealed nature and promises.

Here are some examples of proclamations and requests that bring these realities into our prayers during times of spiritual warfare:

"Ancient of Days, cast down thrones, and send forth Your fiery stream!"

"Open the books of judgment and release Your verdict!"

"Slay the beast. Destroy its body. Let it be given to the burning flame!"

"Let the dominion of evil be taken away and consumed in the fire of Your presence!"

These prayers are not magical formulas. They are scriptural responses to spiritual conflict. When they are spoken in faith and revelation, they activate the Hosts of Heaven. They

> *Heaven has not left the battlefield. Neither should you.*

open the door for God's justice to move swiftly. They remind the enemy, and ourselves, that the Lord of Hosts has not abandoned the battlefield.

This is how we fight: not with fear, but with confidence. Not with isolated strength, but with the backing of an innumerable army. Spiritual warfare becomes an act of alignment, and prayer becomes a channel through which Heaven's warriors are deployed.

We are not alone in the fight. We are not even the frontline. Heaven stands ready. And the multitude is not passive, they are waiting for faith to make room.

Ministry and Evangelism

Among the many areas where the presence of the Angelic Host becomes essential, ministry and evangelism stand out. Whether in pastoral leadership, missions, teaching, prophetic service, or apostolic commissioning, ministry is never a neutral activity. It is, at its core, spiritual warfare. When we step into God's calling, we also step into spiritual conflict.

Assurance: Being a Part of Thousands

This is especially true in difficult or hostile ministry contexts. Evangelism in unreached or resistant environments often confronts not only cultural opposition but spiritual resistance. In such places, the reality of the multitude becomes more than a comforting truth, it becomes a lifeline. The minister may feel outnumbered, unseen, or unsupported. But faith reveals what the eyes cannot see: **"Those who are with us are more than those who are with them"** (2 Kings 6:16).

> *You're not sent empty-handed. You're sent backed by the Host.*

The Angelic Host is not assigned only to protect us, they are also deployed to collaborate with us in the fulfillment of the Great Commission. The Lord of Hosts does not send us alone. He sends us with Heaven's backing. And when we understand this, we learn to pray accordingly.

Before stepping into ministry, especially in unfamiliar, unreached, or dangerous territories, the believer can and should activate Angelic support by faith. This is not superstition. It is biblical partnership.

Scripture reveals that **God manifests Himself with fire** (Psalm 50:3; Isaiah 30:27; Deuteronomy 33:2), and that **Angels are present in His fiery entourage** (Hebrews 12:22; 1 Kings 22:19). This imagery teaches us that wherever God sends us, His Angelic forces accompany His Word and His glory. They are not ornamental. They are active agents in the unfolding of His mission.

Here are examples of prayers that activate this truth:

"Lord, go before me in fire! Let the multitude that is with You go before me. Let them surround me and encamp around my calling!"

"Father, just as the Ancient of Days appears with fire, let Your fiery ones, Your Angels, go ahead into this land, into this meeting, into this mission."

"Let the hills be filled with horses and chariots of fire around Your work."

These declarations do not manipulate God; they align our faith with what He has already promised and revealed. They draw from His Word and posture our hearts to collaborate with Heaven's agenda.

This truth is not merely poetic. It is historical and present.

In **Acts 5:19–20**, an Angel of the Lord bodily released the apostles from prison and gave them instructions to return and preach. In **Daniel 10:12–13**, the Angel Gabriel explained that his mission had been delayed by the prince of Persia and that the archangel Michael came to assist him. In **Revelation 12:7–9**, Michael and his Angels engage in heavenly battle against the dragon and his forces.

Assurance: Being a Part of Thousands

These were not symbolic events. They were real, recorded moments of Angelic intervention in the advancement of God's Word.

And they were not limited to Bible times.

The same Angelic support is available today. It is assigned to every believer walking in obedience to God's purpose. But it must be recognized. It must be believed for. It must be harnessed through prayer and spiritual alignment.

Ministers of the gospel are not solo performers, they are participants in a heavenly mission. And just as Jesus declared in **Matthew 28:18**, *"All authority in heaven and on earth has been given to Me,"* so also does that authority extend to those He sends. That authority is expressed not only through our faith but through the movement of Heaven's Hosts.

> **You are not performing. You are participating-with Heaven.**

The Angelic Host has not been reduced in number. They have not withdrawn their commitment. They have not changed their assignment. But they must be welcomed, invoked, and activated, through a posture of reverent, expectant faith.

Church Life and Community Building

Remember: Angels are sent and serving the community of believers as ministering spirits. (Hebrews 1:14)

The Host isn't just for comfort-it's for community.

The revelation of the angelic multitude is not only a source of personal assurance; it is a powerful model for building and strengthening the Church community. When this truth is taught and practiced within a church body, it fosters unity, support, and a divine sense of collaboration. It offers the Church a vision of itself not just as a human institution but as a spiritual family intimately connected with the Hosts of Heaven.

To integrate this reality into community life, leaders can intentionally cultivate spaces and practices that bring awareness of the multitude into everyday church experience. Church prayers, teaching series, and collaborative community projects can all be shaped by the expectation that the Angelic Host is present and available to assist. These initiatives help the congregation transition from abstract theology to embodied spiritual reality.

Discipleship, by its very nature, is organic and relational. It flourishes through repetition, modeling, and spiritual practices. That is why it is vital for church leaders to organize regular group prayers that focus on the angelic multitudes.

Assurance: Being a Part of Thousands

These communal moments allow members to pray, proclaim, and worship using Scriptures that reveal the presence of Angels. This shared practice strengthens spiritual consciousness and facilitates individual and corporate awareness of the invisible support available to the Church.

Beyond prayer, churches should consider developing teaching series dedicated to the biblical doctrine of Angelic assistance. Chapter 3 of this book can serve as a foundation for such teaching. As the community gains understanding, members will grow in their confidence to trust and rely on God's Hosts in their group efforts. With faith, they will begin to expect Angelic involvement in their ministries, decisions, and local initiatives.

The Word of God affirms this support: *"Are they not all ministering spirits sent forth to minister for them who shall be heirs of salvation?"* (Hebrews 1:14). This verse reminds us that Angels are not a vague presence; they are commissioned servants, assigned to minister on behalf of believers, especially within the gathered Church.

These ministering spirits enhance what the Church alone could not accomplish. The Hosts of Heaven increase the reach, strength, and impact of our human efforts. When the Church embraces this truth, she expands her

> *What the Church cannot carry alone, the Host empowers.*

spiritual capacity, not by striving harder, but by collaborating deeper.

Living Assurance in Action

The practice described above is fertilized through some disciplines that can apply as well to general ways to cultivate connection with the Angelic realm. The process to connect with awareness and relationship with the multitude of Angels sent by the Father at the believer's service is no different but includes a mindfulness of this specific aspect.

Research and meditate.

Living with assurance of the Angelic Host requires more than believing a truth, it requires forming a spiritual posture. That posture begins with intentionally researching and meditating on what God has revealed in His Word. Revelation grows when we give it attention. Faith grows when we root it in Scripture. Meditation creates space for both.

Faith grows when rooted. Meditation is the soil.

The believer who desires to walk in alignment with the multitude must first develop the habit of going to the Scriptures, not just for information, but for transformation. The Bible reveals that God surrounds Himself with a multitude. He works through them, sends them, and aligns them with His will. By studying and internalizing these passages, we gradually open our minds and hearts to the reality of their presence and collaboration.

Research and meditation also prepare the soil of the heart to respond rightly: with gratitude, worship, attentiveness, and faith. They shift us from simply admiring God's power to actually walking in His revealed structure.

This posture unfolds through four simple practices:

> **God works through the multitude-He doesn't work alone.**

a) Meditate

Meditation is the discipline of slowing down. It begins with creating a space of quiet, both externally and internally. In that space, the believer asks the Holy Spirit to bring alive the Word of God.

Start by reading the passage slowly. Ask questions:

- What does this Scripture reveal about the multitude?

- What does it show me about God's ways?

- What stands out in the atmosphere, actions, or words of the Angelic Host?

Then listen. Pay attention to the emotional stirrings, thoughts, and impressions that rise up. Let them lead you into reverence and dialogue with God. Don't rush. Let the Word shape you.

Respond in prayer and worship. Speak what you've seen back to God. Acknowledge what you sense Him emphasizing. The goal is not to analyze Angels, but to become attuned to how their presence reflects God's order, majesty, and mission.

b) Open Your Heart to Be Enlightened by the Holy Spirit and to Grow Your Spiritual Knowledge

The Scriptures do more than instruct, they illuminate. The Holy Spirit brings light where there was once only awareness. As you meditate, ask Him to open the eyes of your heart.

Study how the Angels appear in Scripture:

- In what settings do they appear?

- To whom are they sent?

- What message do they carry?

- What is the atmosphere surrounding their presence?

Observe the character of the people involved. What were they doing before the encounter? How did they respond?

Write down your insights. Keep a dedicated journal for your discoveries. Often, connections will form between passages, people, and patterns. As those patterns emerge, you'll see more clearly how Angels function in partnership with Heaven and how they move among those aligned with God's purpose.

This knowledge, under the Spirit's guidance, does more than inform, it prepares the soul for partnership.

c) Develop Your Faith

Faith is not automatic. It is cultivated. As you meditate and study, begin to **believe** what you're reading. Move from information to trust.

Affirm what the Word says:

- That you are surrounded by the multitude (Hebrews 12:22).

- That Angels are ministering spirits sent for your benefit (Hebrews 1:14).

- That God is the Lord of Hosts, and He acts with them, not without them (Psalm 103:20–21).

Allow these truths to become part of your prayer language and inner dialogue. Declare them over your life.

Also, practice attentiveness throughout the day. Watch for God's movements. Ask, "Could this be a trace of Heaven's activity?" You won't always be certain. But the posture of alertness invites deeper alignment. The more you believe, the more you notice.

<u>Bible Passages</u>

Here are some key Scriptures to meditate on as you grow in awareness of the Angelic Host. These passages will strengthen your theology, ignite your worship, and deepen your assurance.

- **Daniel 7:10** – "A fiery stream issued and came forth from before Him: thousand thousands ministered to Him, and ten thousand times ten thousand stood before Him…"

- **Revelation 5:11** – "Then I looked, and I heard the voice of many Angels…numbering thousands upon thousands, and ten thousand times ten thousand…"

- **Hebrews 1:14** – "Are not all Angels ministering spirits sent to serve those who will inherit salvation?"

- **2 Kings 6:16–17** – "Do not be afraid…those who are with us are more than those who are with them."

- **Psalm 103:20–21** – "Praise the Lord, you his Angels, you mighty ones who do his bidding…"

- **Luke 2:13** – "Suddenly a great company of the heavenly host appeared with the angel…"

- **Hebrews 12:22** – "But you have come to Mount Zion, to the city of the living God, the heavenly Jerusalem. You have come to thousands upon thousands of Angels in joyful assembly."

Make time to read, reflect, and speak these verses aloud. The Word, when meditated upon, will build assurance. And assurance will awaken your cooperation with the multitude.

Develop the culture and habits.

Spiritual assurance deepens not just through moments of revelation but through the development of consistent habits. If we are to live with awareness of the Angelic Host and walk in partnership with them, then we must **build a personal and communal culture that welcomes and sustains that awareness**. This is not achieved through occasional inspiration. It is formed through deliberate rhythms.

The Gate of Number

Culture is the atmosphere we create through repeated values and actions. A Kingdom culture, whether in your personal life, family, or church, grows when truths are reinforced through worship, prayer, study, and shared language. Habits form the structure that sustains this culture.

> *Culture is not what you say-it's what you repeat.*

This means integrating the awareness of the multitude into your spiritual routines. For example:

- As you begin your day, take time to acknowledge the presence of the Lord and His Host.

- In your intercession, thank God for the Angelic assistance He has already provided, and declare your confidence in their presence.

- As you read Scripture, look actively for references to Angels, Hosts, the heavenly assembly, and God's identity as the Lord of Hosts.

- In moments of worship or warfare, intentionally invite Heaven's alignment into your heart, space, and community.

You are not reacting in fear- you are responding with assurance.

These small acts, repeated over time, do something powerful. They retrain your spiritual reflexes. Instead of reacting to challenges from a place of isolation or fear, you begin to respond with assurance: "I am not alone. Heaven is near. The multitude is here."

Just as individuals can develop holy habits, families and faith communities can too. Leaders can set the tone by creating space for reflection on the reality of the Angelic Host in small groups, prayer meetings, or worship environments. When children grow up hearing about the Hosts of the Lord, not as myth, but as part of God's active mission, faith is passed on not only in content but in atmosphere.

Ultimately, culture is what remains when the inspiration fades. If you cultivate it intentionally, it will carry you through moments when your emotions falter. And when your habits reflect the reality of Heaven's multitude, you begin to live from a place of quiet, consistent confidence.

Develop awareness and sensitivity.

Living with the assurance of the multitude is not only about belief, it is about spiritual perception. To walk in alignment with the Angelic Host, believers must **cultivate**

The Gate of Number

awareness and sensitivity to the movements of Heaven. This sensitivity is not mystical in nature, but relational. It is the fruit of a heart trained to recognize the patterns and presence of God.

Pause. Notice. Discern. That's where Heaven becomes visible.

Spiritual awareness begins with attentiveness. Many times, God is present and active, but we miss His activity because our senses are dull or our attention is elsewhere. Developing spiritual sensitivity means learning to pause, to notice, and to discern. It is about retraining the heart and mind to stay alert to what God is doing around and within us.

This awareness is not primarily about seeing Angels physically. Rather, it is about recognizing their presence and action through spiritual discernment, just as Elisha's servant learned to see beyond the visible army to the fiery chariots that surrounded them (2 Kings 6:17). That discernment comes when we ask the Lord to open our eyes, not just once, but as a way of life.

Here are practical ways to develop that kind of awareness:

- Ask daily for the Holy Spirit to sharpen your spiritual perception.

Assurance: Being a Part of Thousands

- Be watchful in prayer. Pay attention to moments when peace enters unexpectedly, when clarity breaks through confusion, or when courage rises without explanation, these may be signs of Heaven's reinforcement.

- Notice atmospheres. Certain places or moments carry an increased sense of divine presence. Learn to respect that. Pause. Ask, "Lord, what are You doing here?"

Sensitivity also means learning to respond. When you sense God's nearness or a stirring in your spirit, do not dismiss it. Acknowledge it in prayer. Give thanks. Lean in. Obedience is often the doorway to increased perception.

> *Perception begins with obedience.*

Over time, this practice trains your inner man. You begin to walk with a sense of sacred companionship. You become more aware not only of God's Spirit, but of His organized movement through the Angelic Host. Your language begins to reflect this awareness. Your prayers carry new boldness. And your posture before God becomes one of reverent attentiveness.

This is not reserved for prophets or mystics. It is part of what it means to be a disciple. Jesus told His followers, *"Blessed are your eyes because they see, and your ears because they hear"*

The Gate of Number

(Matthew 13:16). That blessing is still offered today, for those who ask, who wait, and who walk in awareness.

Develop intentionality

Spiritual awareness must be paired with intentional action. What we perceive about the presence of the Angelic Host must shape how we choose to live. Assurance grows when our mindset, language, and habits consistently reflect the reality we believe. That is why cultivating intentionality is a vital discipline for walking in partnership with the multitude.

Intentionality means choosing to live as though the Angelic Host is truly present, because they are. It means speaking, praying, and ministering with the understanding that God has surrounded you with a company far greater than what your natural eyes can see.

This starts in the mind. Each day, set your thoughts in alignment with this truth. Remind yourself:

"I am not alone. I am part of a multitude. Heaven walks with me."

Awareness doesn't make us arrogant-it makes us faithful.

This posture is not meant to make us presumptuous, it is meant to make us faithful. It leads us to listen more carefully to the Spirit, to speak more

Assurance: Being a Part of Thousands

confidently in prayer, and to walk with greater steadiness in trials. When you are intentional about your awareness, your atmosphere changes.

Your speech should also reflect this intentionality. Begin to affirm what the Word says about the Host of Heaven. Declare aloud the truths you've meditated on:

- "The Lord is with me as the Lord of Hosts."

- "Thousands upon thousands surround His throne and carry out His will."

- "They are ministering spirits sent to serve the heirs of salvation, and I am one of them." (Hebrews 1:14)

Let these declarations become part of your language of faith. Let them train your emotions, renew your mindset, and anchor your confidence.

Intentionality also includes how you make decisions. Before entering a meeting, praying for someone, or stepping into spiritual responsibility, pause. Ask God:

"Father, let Your Hosts surround this moment. Let Your Angels stand at my side. Let me act in agreement with Heaven's design."

The Gate of Number

Such prayers are not superstitious, they are relational. They reveal a heart that walks with Heaven's rhythm.

This kind of intentional living trains your soul to walk in assurance. You begin to face trials with greater calm, lead with greater confidence, and pray with greater expectation. You stop reacting to life as though you are outnumbered. Instead, you begin responding from the conviction that Heaven is always near, and that its multitude moves with those who walk in covenant.

DEPLOYING THE MULTITUDE.

It is not enough to believe in the multitude. To fully walk in the assurance of their presence, we must also learn to **deploy** them, intentionally releasing the Hosts of Heaven into the areas of our lives where their help is needed. This is not about commanding Angels by our own will. It is about aligning ourselves with God's purposes and activating their ministry through faith, discernment, and Spirit-led prayer.

> *Don't just believe in the multitude-learn to walk with them.*

Assurance: Being a Part of Thousands

> *Angels don't improvise. They carry instruction and fulfill purpose.*

The Angelic Host is already assigned to serve God's people. But their action is most visible and impactful when believers learn how to welcome, activate, and cooperate with them through understanding and spiritual sensitivity.

Here are practical ways to deploy the multitude:

a) Grow in Knowledge and Confidence

You must first grow in your understanding of the Hosts of Heaven. Learn what Scripture says about their nature, their assignments, and how they function in the fulfillment of God's will. The more you understand, the more confident you become.

Confidence does not mean presumption. It means knowing the character of God and the order of His Kingdom. Angels serve Him, not us, but they are sent for us (Hebrews 1:14). That is a privilege we should not neglect.

b) Increase in Sensitivity to the Holy Spirit

Deploying the multitude begins with discerning God's heart and leading in a given situation. Ask the Holy Spirit:

- "What are You doing in this moment?"

- "What is Heaven's position concerning this situation?"

- "Where do You want me to invite Your reinforcement?"

The Hosts of Heaven move in unity with the Spirit. When you increase in your sensitivity to Him, you also become more synchronized with the operations of Heaven.

c) Respond in Faith through Spoken Prayer

Once you've sensed the Lord's desire, respond with words of faith. Faith-filled prayer is one of the clearest biblical ways to activate Angelic engagement. Scripture is filled with examples where prayer opened doors for Angelic intervention (Daniel 10:12–13, Acts 12:5–10).

Declare what you believe. Speak what the Word affirms. Ask boldly for the Lord of Hosts to command His Angels concerning the matter at hand. This is how prayer becomes a bridge between revelation and deployment.

d) Respond in Faith through Prophetic Action

Sometimes, faith requires movement. A prophetic action might be something simple, standing in a room, anointing a doorpost, laying hands, or proclaiming a scripture aloud in a space, . When done under the Spirit's leading, such actions release alignment in the atmosphere.

It is not the act itself that moves Angels, but the faith and obedience behind it. Just as praise and obedience invite the Spirit's presence, prophetic acts under God's direction can create a landing space for Angelic operation.

e) Be Strategic in Moments of Crisis or High Calling

There are moments when warfare intensifies, decisions carry long-term weight, or opportunities emerge that require great courage. In these moments, be deliberate.

Say aloud:

- "Father, let the multitude be deployed."
- "Let Your Angelic Host be sent into this battle, into this meeting, into this territory."

The Gate of Number

- "As the Lord of Hosts, stretch out Your hand, and release those who excel in strength to fulfill Your Word." (Psalm 103:20)

In high-pressure environments, ministry trips, evangelistic events, personal crisis, major transitions, ask God specifically for Angelic support. He is willing. The Hosts are ready. And faith is the key that opens the way.

The Hosts are ready. Faith is the key. Ask.

The multitude is not a metaphor. They are messengers, warriors, worshippers, and enforcers of God's will. They are not to be worshipped, but they are to be honored, welcomed, and deployed in partnership with the purposes of God on the earth.

INTEGRATING THE REVELATION OF THE MULTITUDE IN YOUR PRAYER LIFE.

To walk in full assurance, you must do more than study and believe the truth about the multitude, you must pray with it. When the revelation of the Angelic Host becomes part of your prayer life, it begins to shape your spiritual posture, deepen your communion with God, and align your petitions with Heaven's reality.

Assurance: Being a Part of Thousands

This is not about praying to Angels. Scripture is clear, worship and prayer are directed to God alone. But it is about learning to pray with awareness of their presence, and in alignment with the truths Scripture reveals about how they move in God's service. It is about praying with the confidence that Heaven is not silent, and you are not alone.

Pray in alignment-not to the Angels, but with them.

The Psalms offer us rich examples of this kind of prayer. Consider the way David and other psalmists called upon the Hosts of Heaven in worship and proclamation:

"Bless the Lord, O you His Angels, you mighty ones who do His word, obeying the voice of His word! Bless the Lord, all His Hosts, His ministers, who do His will!"

(Psalm 103:20–21)

"God will give you His Angels charge over you, to guard you in all your ways."

(Psalm 91:11)

In prayer, you can echo these words. You can take your stand within these truths. You can speak Scripture aloud, not only as affirmation, but as active agreement with Heaven's operation.

The Gate of Number

In addition, you can learn to identify with the kinds of prayers prayed by those who experienced the revelation of the multitude in Scripture. You can:

- Join Daniel in crying out, "O Ancient of Days, let the thrones be cast down!" (Daniel 7:9–10).

- Join the psalmists in blessing the Lord among the Hosts.

- Join Elisha in declaring, *"There are more with us than with them"* (2 Kings 6:16).

- Join the writer of Hebrews in rejoicing that you have *"come to Mount Zion… and to myriads of Angels in joyful assembly"* (Hebrews 12:22).

Let these truths become part of your intercession. When you pray for healing, breakthrough, or justice, remember: God often sends His word, and He sends His Angels to fulfill it (Psalm 103:20).

Awareness of Angels shapes the atmosphere of our gatherings.

When praying for others, visualize their need not as isolated, but as fully covered by the presence of the Host. Ask the Lord:

Assurance: Being a Part of Thousands

Let the multitude stand with them. Let Your Angels minister to them, protect them, surround them. Let Your will be done with the strength of Heaven.

In times of danger or uncertainty, pray with confidence:

Lord of Hosts, You are not absent. Send forth those who excel in strength. Let the multitude move in this moment. Let what is hidden be revealed. Let what is broken be lifted.

Prayer like this is not about emotional hype, it is about spiritual agreement. You are not praying for fantasy. You are praying with truth.

When this becomes part of your language of faith, it does more than inform your prayers, it transforms your perspective. You begin to see the world differently. You begin to stand more firmly. You begin to worship with deeper joy. You no longer pray as someone hoping for help, you pray as someone standing among Heaven's army.

You have come to Mount Zion.

You have come to the city of the living God.

You have come to myriads of Angels.

So pray like it.

This is the kind of assurance God wants for every believer. Not the kind that comes from positive thinking, but

The Gate of Number

the kind rooted in revealed truth, the kind that walks boldly because Heaven is not empty.

You are not abandoned.

You are not forgotten.

You are not outnumbered.

You are part of thousands.

And they are part of you.

So live with confidence.

Pray with conviction.

Serve with strength.

Stand in the fire if you must, knowing that others stood before you, and that you are not standing alone.

Heaven is not empty.

And because of that, neither is your calling.

The Day They Saw the Angels

(A True Story as Told by the Author)

Assurance: Being a Part of Thousands

I read the story of a university professor from Massachusetts, a thoughtful, disciplined man, not given to spiritual sensationalism. His faith was sincere but steady, rooted more in study than in emotion. But one day… (as he shared his story, one will easily sense the reverence of someone who had encountered something holy.)

He and his wife had gone for a walk in the woods near their home. It was a quiet, ordinary afternoon. But as they stepped into a clearing, something shifted. The atmosphere became still, so still it felt charged. And then, they saw them.

"They weren't imaginary," he told me. "They were radiant, upright, and filled with peace. We didn't hear words, but we knew they were speaking. Their presence said everything."

For several moments, the couple stood in awe, completely overtaken by the sense that they were not alone. The beings before them glowed with light, not harsh, but weighty. Then, as gently as they had come, they faded from sight.

"We never talk about it lightly," the professor shared. "It wasn't a vision. It wasn't a dream. It was real. And it changed everything."

He explained that after that encounter, prayer felt different. Scripture felt fuller. Even the challenges of life felt smaller, not because life was easier, but because his sense of God's presence had expanded.

"I used to pray like I was asking help from far away," he said. "Now I pray like I'm surrounded, because I am."

This story is not offered to suggest that all believers will see the Angelic Host visibly. That is God's decision. But it is a reminder that what we've explored in this chapter is not symbolic or abstract. It is real. It is near. And it is meant to be lived.

Walking in the Assurance of Angelic Support

You are not walking alone-you are walking accompanied.

Living out the revelation of angelic support is not an optional add-on to our spiritual journey, it is an integral part of how God intends for us to live with confidence, strength, and clarity of purpose. This truth is not only rooted in Scripture but designed for active engagement. As we have seen, the multitude of Angels is real, organized, and constantly involved in God's plan, not only on a cosmic scale but in the minute details of our lives and ministries.

Throughout this chapter, we explored how assurance comes from understanding that we are not alone, neither in spiritual warfare, ministry, moments of weakness, nor in our

Assurance: Being a Part of Thousands

calling. Whether we are crying out for help in personal struggle or boldly advancing the mission of God in evangelism, the Host of Heaven is near.

We have seen that Angels are not passive observers. They are "ministering spirits, sent forth to serve those who will inherit salvation" (Hebrews 1:14). They carry out divine assignments and partner with those who walk in covenant with God. They respond to faith. They align with the Word of God. And they amplify the effectiveness of the Church when we pray and serve with the awareness of their presence.

This reality is not meant to remain abstract or distant. It is meant to reshape how we think, how we pray, and how we lead. You are not just a believer trying to make it through life. You are part of the multitude, and the multitude walks with you.

Chapter 7
To Meditate Further

- Where in my life do I feel alone—and how might the awareness of the Host shift my posture?

- What would change in my confidence and calling if I truly believed I am not only sent—but accompanied?

- How does the biblical image of the multitude of Angels challenge my view of God's provision and presence?

- What small or private acts might carry greater weight if I saw them as happening

- What practical actions can church leaders take to integrate the revelation of angelic support into community life?

(2 Kings 6:16–17; Hebrews 12:1; Matthew 26:53; Psalm 91:11–12; Luke 15:10; Daniel 7:10; Acts 27:23–24)

VIII

Humility: The call of the incomprehensible

And I John saw these things, and heard them. And when I had heard and seen, I fell down to worship before the feet of the angel which shewed me these things. Then saith he unto me, See thou do it not: for I am thy fellowservant, and of thy brethren the prophets, and of them which keep the sayings of this book: worship God.
Revelation 22:8-9

The Gate of Number

Chapter 8 calls us to the posture that makes heavenly collaboration possible: humility. This final chapter shows that walking with the Angelic Host requires not superiority but alignment-a heart low enough to trust what it cannot fully comprehend. As God's design unfolds through mystery, complexity, and the unseen, humility becomes our safeguard and our gateway. This chapter teaches how to embrace divine incomprehensibility without fear, how to welcome angelic help without pride, and how to root confidence in God's wisdom rather than human understanding. Step by step, it guides readers to cultivate a humility that listens, yields, discerns, honors, and obeys-even when the path is unclear. As practical as it is spiritual, this chapter shows how humility makes space for God to act through us and around us-through the visible and the invisible, with the help of thousands.

CHAPTER 8

HUMILITY: THE CALL OF THE INCOMPREHENSIBLE

WALKING IN COLLABORATION WITH THE ANGELIC HOSTS: HUMILITY IN ACTION

The more we grasp the structure and movement of Heaven, the more we realize that partnership with the Angelic Hosts is not only powerful, it is deeply humbling. Walking in collaboration with the multitude of Heaven invites us into a posture of reverence and smallness, not because we are insignificant, but because God is infinitely majestic and His ways far surpass our own.

This humility is not weakness. It is clarity. It comes from knowing our place in the great unfolding of God's will. The Hosts of Heaven, who excel in strength and wisdom, walk in complete obedience, not out of compulsion, but from understanding who God is. They move at His command, worship without ceasing, and serve with unwavering joy. To collaborate with such beings requires more than boldness, it requires surrender. It requires humility.

> *True collaboration with Heaven begins with surrender, not strength.*

Humility, in this context, is not just a personal virtue; it is the essential atmosphere of true collaboration. Without it, we will either shrink away from God's invitation out of insecurity or try to grasp at divine power through pride. But with humility, we are able to take our rightful place, not above, not beneath, but in harmony with God's intention.

It is this posture that allows us to be effective in the Great Commission. When we learn to collaborate with the Angelic Hosts, we do not command them; we align with the One who sends them. We do not strive to manipulate spiritual realities; we learn to submit to the rhythm of God's Kingdom. That submission is what gives birth to fruitfulness. It is the inner shift that prepares us to steward the extraordinary with reverent obedience.

As we begin this final chapter of Part 2, we are reminded that Heaven's greatness is not there to intimidate us, it is there to invite us. The invitation is not to rise above our humanity, but to walk humbly within it, in the power of the Spirit and in collaboration with the Hosts of Heaven. This is the call of humility: to know who we are, to accept who we are not, and to rejoice in the privilege of partnering with God in a way that both honors His greatness and embraces our own sacred role.

Human Response to Complexity

Human beings have always responded to complexity with a mix of creativity and vulnerability. Whether it is the intricacy of the natural world, the paradoxes of faith, or the realities of Angelic collaboration, we each bring unique reactions, shaped by our personalities, cultures, and spiritual formation. These reactions are not just mental or intellectual; they often emerge as deep emotional experiences.

For some, complexity brings confusion, like walking through a dense fog, unsure of direction. Others respond with fear, unnerved by the uncertainties they cannot control. Insecurity surfaces when people feel inadequate in the face of overwhelming information. Frustration bubbles up when minds struggle to grasp the intricate truths unfolding before them.

But these are not the only responses. In seeking to manage what feels too vast, people often fall into common behavioral patterns. Some simplify the complex to make it more manageable, reducing mystery to formulas. Others choose avoidance, ignoring what feels unreachable. Some hesitate, paralyzed by the weight of the unknown, while others turn to experimentation, trying to navigate trial and error. Still others lean into collaboration, pooling insights in hope of collective clarity. And sometimes, we resist, pushing back against what threatens our sense of control.

Yet even in this range of reactions, positive responses emerge. Complexity can stir awe, drawing us into reverence. It can spark a thirst for knowledge, pushing us to study, question, and grow. It can encourage adaptation, inviting us to develop new ways of thinking and living.

> **When the mystery is too vast, humility is the only way forward.**

However, our response to complexity ultimately depends on the posture of our heart. When we encounter something greater than ourselves, we have two choices. We can yield to despair, calling our limitations defeat, or we can choose humility, and allow those limitations to become fertile ground for surrender and transformation.

For the believer, this is a sacred invitation.

When we face the vastness of God's design, including the profound realities of the Angelic Host, we are not meant to be crushed by the incomprehensible. We are meant to be led into deeper humility. We are invited to trust what we cannot control, and to walk with what we do not fully understand. This is not passive surrender. It is the posture of partnership. The Hosts of Heaven do not serve because they know everything, they serve because they trust the One who does.

God's Word confirms that there are things He has chosen to keep hidden and things He has chosen to reveal. *"The secret things belong to the Lord our God, but the things revealed belong to us and to our children forever"* (Deuteronomy 29:29). Humility teaches us how to live within this boundary, not resenting the unknown, but honoring it.

> *Humility doesn't resent mystery-it reveres it.*

This attitude becomes essential as we learn to collaborate with Angels. Their ways reflect the unsearchable wisdom of God. And while we are not given every detail, we are given access. When we adopt the posture of humility, we become receptive to their support, not through analysis, but through alignment.

To cultivate this posture:

- Begin by acknowledging that you will never know everything.

- Let this acceptance shift you from frustration to curiosity, from insecurity to wonder.

- Embrace the unknown as God's tool to draw you into trust, not as a barrier to be overcome.

As the prophet Isaiah reminds us:

The Gate of Number

"Fear not, for I am with you; be not dismayed, for I am your God. I will strengthen you, I will help you, I will uphold you with my righteous right hand" (Isaiah 41:10).

This trust becomes a doorway to deeper relationship with God, and deeper fellowship with others. Humility opens space for collaboration. It allows us to recognize that someone else may carry insight we do not yet possess. And as this trust grows, gratitude becomes our lens, replacing the anxiety of the unknown with thanksgiving for what has been revealed.

Humility isn't passive-it's power in its proper place.

Humility is not weakness. It is strength rightly placed. It is the conscious decision to prioritize learning over ego. It teaches us to navigate spiritual mystery with resilience, to engage divine reality with empathy, and to pursue the things of God with wisdom rather than pride.

Above all, humility in the face of mystery is the mark of spiritual maturity. It frees us from needing to control what God never asked us to explain. It roots us in the truth that divine complexity is not meant to destroy, it is designed to draw us closer.

Even the majestic structure of the Angelic Host, in all its complexity and magnitude, is not a threat, it is an expression of God's order and help. The Hosts do not stand above us in condemnation. They stand with us, sent to help us fulfill the mission of Heaven.

We are not excluded from that mystery. We are invited into it, not to understand it fully, but to walk with confidence in the One who holds it all.

The features of the virtue of humility

The Practical Features of Humility

As we have seen, humility is the appropriate response to the vast complexity of God's design, especially as it relates to the Angelic Host and the spiritual structures of Heaven. But humility is more than an inner feeling or theological principle; it expresses itself in real attitudes and daily behaviors. It creates an atmosphere in which revelation can grow and divine collaboration becomes possible.

Here are five key traits that mark the life of someone walking in the virtue of humility:

- **Open-Mindedness**

Humble people remain open to new ideas, fresh perspectives, and unfamiliar experiences. They know that

Humble wisdom listens more than it speaks.

their current understanding, while valuable, is incomplete. True wisdom listens. *"Let the wise listen and add to their learning,"* says Proverbs 1:5, and again, *"Instruct the wise and they will be wiser still"* (Proverbs 9:9). Openness is not naivety, it is the courage to keep learning.

- **Curiosity**

Humility fuels curiosity. Instead of being threatened by what they don't know, humble people lean in with wonder. They ask questions. They pursue truth. They are not ashamed to be learners. Proverbs 18:15 reminds us: *"The heart of the discerning acquires knowledge, for the ears of the wise seek it out."*

- **Respect for Others**

A humble person honors the dignity and experience of others. They do not assume superiority but recognize that everyone carries insights shaped by their journey. Romans 12:10 urges us to *"Be devoted to one another in love. Honor one another above yourselves."* Humility listens and learns through dialogue, knowing that community refines our understanding.

- **Resilience**

> *The humble endure-not because they have all answers, but because they trust God's process.*

Humility enables strength, not in domination, but in endurance. It grants grace in the face of ambiguity and patience in the face of uncertainty. As James encourages: *"Let perseverance finish its work so that you may be mature and complete, not lacking anything"* (James 1:4). The humble endure not because they have every answer, but because they trust God's process.

- **Spiritual Depth**

At its core, humility is spiritual. It reflects maturity, reverence, and surrender. Isaiah 66:2 declares: *"These are the ones I look on with favor: those who are humble and contrite in spirit, and who tremble at my word."* Humble people hold God's Word with awe. They do not rush to master it; they allow it to master them.

These features may seem simple, but they are powerful. They create a spiritual ecosystem where pride dies, wisdom grows, and God's presence is welcomed. They prepare the believer to recognize the movements of Heaven, not with fear, but with readiness. And they build the inner posture needed for the next step in our journey: learning how humility grants access to the higher mysteries of divine revelation.

Humility in the understanding of Heavenly entities

As Christians, the concept of humility in the face of what we cannot fully comprehend takes on a profound significance when it comes to understanding heavenly things and the Heavenly Hosts.

The very first reality to which those values would be applied to, is towards the 'Word of God'. This type of humility prompts us to submit ourselves to the authority of divine revelation as conveyed in Scripture. While the Bible reveals much about God, heaven, and the angelic realm, it also acknowledges the limitations of human language and comprehension when it comes to describing these realities and moreover humans' capacity to comprehend it. Humility allows us to approach the Bible with a childlike trust. It recognizes first that what is said in the sacred Scripture is true as said. This looks like a simplistic statement. And that is exactly what it is. Its simplistic nature is not meant to dismiss the hard historical and textual criticism endeavors, they are similarly valuable. The apparent tension that appears finds simple resolution in the mystery of humble surrender which many have experienced. This posture recognizes that as genuine and relevant that our human efforts are, our ability to fully grasp Heaven does not depend on them, ultimately, but on God. We would neither yield to skepticism nor be consumed by a non-surrendered drive to fully understand every aspect of these realities. Humility invites us to approach them with reverence and wonder. Humility is thus measured first in relation to a person's trust and surrender to God and His Word and toward divine wisdom. It is because it derives from that source that its expression is made true and fruitful. This attitude of humility acknowledges the vastness and majesty of God's creation and gain access to its multiplexity.

> *Humility opens wonder, not worry, in the face of Heaven's mysteries.*

Humility reminds us to trust in the wisdom and goodness of the Almighty. It urges us to surrender our doubts and uncertainties and take confidence in the providential care of God as expressed through the good words He stated. We may stumble in our attempts to comprehend heavenly mysteries and may not fully comprehend the nature of Heavenly Hosts. However, we can trust that God works all things according to His perfect wisdom. (Isaiah 55:8-9). This attitude does not stagnate in complacency; rather, it motivates the seeker to remain a continual learner in his existential journey and faith. We recognize that our understanding of heavenly realities may deepen over time as we grow in our relationship with God and comprehension of His Word.

The Gate of Number

Humility lived in the sanctuary of prayer leads the seeker in worship as a response to the mysteries of heaven. In prayer, the seeker seeks God's guidance and insights, trusting in His Spirit to illuminate his heart and minds with increasing understanding. He embraces his finite understanding in the presence of His infinite intelligence. These features are not strange to Angel's character and conduct. They, actually, are heavenly decorum.

The Spiritual Posture of Humility Before Divine Mystery

The practice of humility does not end with behavior, it deepens into posture. Beyond open-mindedness and curiosity, humility takes its fullest form when we stand before God's mystery and choose to surrender rather than strive. This is where humility becomes spiritual strength.

There will always be truths in the Christian life that stretch beyond our understanding. The Scriptures themselves speak to this. *"The secret things belong to the Lord our God, but the things revealed belong to us and to our children forever"* (Deuteronomy 29:29). In other words, God has given us revelation, but He has also retained mystery. The humble learn to live within that boundary, not with anxiety, but with reverence.

Some things are hidden for our safety. Humility honors the boundary.

Humility: The Call of the Incomprehensible

This is the spiritual posture that allows us to receive what God gives and release what He has not yet explained. It is the posture that opens our spirit to Heaven's movement. Without it, even revelation becomes distorted. With it, even mystery becomes fruitful.

This matters especially when we consider our response to the Word of God. Humility calls us to receive Scripture not as one voice among many, but as the revealed heart and will of God. We are invited to submit, not as those who are intellectually weak, but as those who trust the wisdom of a higher authority. When Scripture presents truth that feels simple or unsearchable, we do not explain it away. We bow before it, allowing it to reshape our thinking.

That does not mean we discard tools like textual analysis or historical research. These can be useful for study. But they are not the final judge of truth. The humble heart does not place its trust in cleverness. It places its trust in the Author. This is why childlike faith so often carries more spiritual clarity than academic brilliance. It is not anti-intellectual, it is spiritually aligned.

> **Revelation comes not through brilliance, but through trust in the Author.**

This humility becomes essential when we seek to understand the Heavenly dimension, especially the structure, presence, and purpose of the Angelic Host. While the Bible

The Gate of Number

gives us glimpses, it does not give exhaustive detail. That, too, is by design. God has given us enough to trust Him, to honor His order, and to walk in collaboration. But He has also preserved mystery so that we remain dependent on Him rather than on our frameworks.

The humble receive this design with gratitude. They are not overwhelmed by the unknown. They are empowered by what has been made known. They trust that God's created structures, including the vastness of the Angelic Host, are not meant to intimidate, but to support us. They do not shrink from the spiritual realm. They lean in, anchored in the conviction that God is good, and that what He has ordained is for our flourishing.

This posture also reframes how we deal with our own limitations. We are not meant to know everything. Our minds were not built to contain the cosmos. That limitation is not a flaw, it is an invitation to depend. It is a call to **reverence**, not retreat. And it reminds us that Heaven's strength is made perfect not in human certainty, but in surrendered trust.

Such humility also reshapes how we relate to others. It makes us listeners. It helps us honor voices and perspectives we may not fully understand. It teaches us to ask questions, to invite dialogue, to recognize that others may carry insights we do not yet possess. This openness prepares the Church to walk not just with one another, but in communion with the Hosts of Heaven.

Humility: The Call of the Incomprehensible

Gratitude is one of humility's most beautiful fruits. Rather than complaining about what is unclear, the humble give thanks for what God has revealed. This spirit of gratitude fosters worship, steadies the soul, and draws us into alignment with the culture of Heaven, where Angels themselves worship not because they know everything, but because they know the One who does.

Gratitude is the language of the humble.

Humility is not a detour from understanding. It is the way into it. It shifts us from control to surrender, from striving to listening. It makes room for divine revelation. And it prepares our hearts to **recognize, receive, and collaborate with the Heavenly Host** not through striving, but through reverence.

THE CHARACTER OF CONNECTION

Humility doesn't pull away-it pulls us together.

Humility does not isolate, it connects. Once cultivated as a personal virtue and spiritual posture, humility naturally leads us outward. It opens the way to deeper relationship: with God, with others, and with the unseen structures of Heaven. It's not just about bowing low, it's about walking together.

The Gate of Number

This connection is both horizontal and vertical. Horizontally, it shapes how we relate to people, embracing community, adaptability, and spiritual sensitivity. Vertically, it influences how we engage with God's invisible Kingdom, including our partnership with the Angelic Host.

Let's explore the path humility creates toward authentic connection. Each step is practical and transformational, grounded in how we live and how we relate.

Fellowship and Community

Practice active humility in your community by choosing to listen more than you speak, honor others' contributions before asserting your own, and regularly affirm your need for shared spiritual growth.

Humility strengthens the foundation of authentic fellowship. The humble person is not driven by self-importance, comparison, or performance. Instead, they bring a posture of service, listening, and shared journey. In a world that often rewards self-promotion, humility becomes a quiet rebellion that makes space for others.

This spirit is essential to any faith community. Fellowship is not just shared activity; it is the mutual recognition that we need each other. When we walk in humility, we no longer try to prove

> *Humility stops trying to prove itself-and starts making room for others.*

we are enough on our own. We accept that God often reveals Himself through others, and that we are formed through the relationships He gives us.

In a humble community:

- People listen more than they speak.

- They celebrate one another's gifts rather than compete.

- They carry one another's burdens, knowing they may one day need the same grace in return.

This posture also prepares the community to walk in spiritual partnership, not only with one another, but with Heaven. When a church or group honors God's order and walks humbly with each other, the Angelic Host is more freely released among them.

> *Heaven moves where humility makes space.*

Unity draws the presence of God. Humility attracts Heaven's movement.

The Gate of Number

True fellowship is not casual or convenient, it is covenantal. And it flourishes when humility becomes the common ground. The result is not just a connected people, but a people who are ready to connect with the purposes of God on a much larger scale.

Flexibility and Adaptability:

Practice adaptability by holding your plans loosely before God, asking daily: "Lord, where are You leading today, and how can I flex to follow You well?"

Humility makes us flexible. When we are not clinging to control or fixated on being right, we become more responsive to what God is doing, even when it surprises us. The humble heart is adaptable because it trusts that God can lead through change, redirect plans, and reveal truth in stages.

The humble heart flexes because it trusts.

Spiritual maturity is not marked by rigidity, but by responsiveness. The proud resist change because it threatens their sense of competence. The humble, however, understand that growth requires movement, and movement requires the willingness to be adjusted.

In a world filled with shifting circumstances, and in a Kingdom where God's ways are often higher than ours, adaptability is essential. God rarely operates within our fixed assumptions. His guidance may come through unexpected people, in unfamiliar ways, or in timings we didn't anticipate. And His Angelic Host, though structured and ordered, move with divine precision that may not follow human routines.

> **When plans shift, the humble pivot with Heaven.**

Humility equips us to flow with these rhythms. Instead of panicking when plans shift or outcomes unfold differently than expected, the humble seek God's presence in the pivot. They ask, "Lord, how are You moving now? And how do I align with You here?"

This posture also prepares us for effective partnership with the Hosts of Heaven. Just as Angels move at God's command without hesitation, the humble learn to yield without delay when God calls them into new spaces or strategies.

Sensitivity to Spiritual Realities:

Practice spiritual sensitivity by cultivating daily moments of quiet where you ask the Holy Spirit, "What am I missing?", and then wait in silence to listen.

The Gate of Number

> *Humility opens the senses that pride keeps shut.*

Humility sharpens our sensitivity to the spiritual world. A heart that is surrendered and teachable becomes more attuned to the presence, promptings, and priorities of the Spirit. It learns to recognize the invisible movements of God, both in personal moments and in the wider unfolding of His purposes.

Those who are proud tend to reduce everything to logic, visibility, and control. But humility allows us to sense what cannot always be explained. It opens our spiritual senses, our ability to perceive divine activity beyond what the eye can see or the mind can immediately grasp.

This kind of sensitivity is essential for walking in awareness of the Angelic Host. Angels are spirit-beings. They do not always appear visibly, but they are actively present and participating in God's mission. Without humility, we miss their movements, not because they are absent, but because we are closed. The humble, however, discern their activity through prayer, worship, Scripture, and a heart positioned in quiet awareness.

> *The Hosts are not far-but pride can close our eyes.*

Jesus consistently demonstrated this sensitivity. He responded to the Father in ways that surprised others because

He was attuned to a reality they did not see. Likewise, if we want to walk in step with Heaven, we must grow in this spiritual alertness. This is not about being mystical, it is about being responsive.

A humble person will often pause and ask:

- "Lord, is there more happening here than I see?"
- "What do You want me to perceive?"
- "What is Heaven doing in this moment?"

Such questions signal a posture of spiritual attentiveness, a willingness to tune in, rather than rush ahead.

Faith and Trust:

Practice humility through trust by saying daily: "Lord, I may not see everything, but I trust that You are working through everything, and I will follow You anyway."

At the heart of humility lies faith, faith that trusts God even when we do not understand. Humility does not demand immediate clarity. It does not insist on proofs or explanations before obedience. Instead, it leans into the character of God, confident that He is good, wise,

Humility walks forward even when the light is dim.

The Gate of Number

and always present, even when circumstances or revelations feel incomplete.

Trust is what allows us to rest when we cannot control. It frees us to follow God through uncertainty, to believe His promises when we don't yet see their fulfillment, and to wait patiently when His timeline does not match our own.

This kind of faith is not passive. It is deeply active. It shows up in how we pray, how we respond to disruption, and how we endure trials. Faith doesn't pretend to have all the answers. It simply chooses to believe that God does.

> **Faith doesn't need all the answers-just the right Person.**

This is especially vital when relating to the spiritual realm, where the logic of Heaven often runs counter to human reasoning. The structures of the Angelic Host, their roles in our lives, and their timing in God's mission are not always clear to us. But they are aligned with divine wisdom. The humble believer chooses to trust that alignment, even when it is unseen.

When we trust, we stop striving. We pray with confidence, even when the outcome is still in process. We act with boldness, even when our path is not fully lit. We open the door to collaborate with God and with His messengers, because we believe, deeply, that He who calls us is faithful (1 Thessalonians 5:24).

Conducts to Grow as We Walk the Path

Humility is not a destination; it is a journey. As we walk the path of divine collaboration, especially in partnership with the Angelic Host, humility becomes both our posture and our companion. And like all virtues, it grows with practice.

The previous section explored the relational and spiritual expressions of humility. Now we turn to the steps that help us develop it, intentionally and progressively. These practices are not abstract, they are walkable. They shape how we grow in grace, discernment, and spiritual cooperation with Heaven.

Here are seven ways we grow as we walk in humility.

1. Praying for Humility and Guidance

Growth begins with asking. Prayer is the doorway to humility because it acknowledges our dependence. When we ask God to shape our hearts, we declare that we cannot transform ourselves. We need Him.

Humility begins on our knees- with a prayer, not a plan.

Ask boldly and consistently:

- "Lord, teach me to be humble."

- "Form in me a heart that listens, yields, and obeys."

- "Lead me in Your wisdom, and guide my steps in truth."

God is eager to answer such prayers. When we ask for humility, He will often bring moments that reveal our weakness, not to shame us, but to free us from the illusion of self-sufficiency. These moments, though sometimes uncomfortable, become holy ground for transformation.

Guidance, too, is part of this prayer. The humble know they need direction, not just general wisdom, but specific leading from the Holy Spirit. The more we ask, the more we become attuned. And as our hearts are softened, we will begin to recognize when God sends insight, through His Word, through His Spirit, and even through His Angelic messengers.

Practice humility today by beginning your prayers with the words: "Lord, I need You to shape my heart and lead my steps, I cannot do this without You."

2. Embracing Mystery and Trusting God's Plan

Humility matures as we learn to accept what we cannot explain. Not every truth will come with full understanding. Not every divine movement will carry immediate clarity. Yet the humble heart does not panic in the face of mystery, it leans into trust.

> *God speaks mystery. We answer with trust.*

God has never promised to reveal everything. Instead, He calls us to walk by faith, knowing that *"His ways are higher than our ways"* (Isaiah 55:9). Mystery, then, is not an obstacle, it is an invitation. It draws us into deeper dependence, deeper worship, and deeper reverence for the One who sees the whole picture.

This principle is vital when we think about the Angelic Host. Their operations are ordered, but not always observable. Their assignments are strategic, but not always understood. The humble person resists the urge to control or demand. Instead, they surrender to the wisdom of God's plan, trusting that what is hidden is still holy.

Such surrender requires more than intellectual agreement, it calls for emotional trust. It means saying:

- "Lord, I don't need to understand everything to follow You."

The Gate of Number

- "I trust that You are good, even in the gaps."

- "I will walk forward, not because I know the full path, but because I know Your character."

Mystery does not diminish God's goodness; it reveals it. And humility enables us to rest in that goodness while the details remain unseen.

Practice embracing mystery today by saying aloud, "God, I trust You even when I do not understand, Your plan is wiser than my explanation."

3. Trusting in God's Wisdom for the Unseen

There is much more to reality than what we can observe. The visible world is only part of God's creation. The Scriptures tell us plainly that **the unseen realm is just as active, just as ordered, and just as essential** as what we perceive with our natural senses (Hebrews 11:3). And humility is what opens us to trust God in that unseen dimension.

Humility opens the eyes to the world we cannot see.

When we consider the Angelic Host, this truth becomes especially relevant. We don't always see their actions, hear their voices, or track their assignments. Yet the humble heart learns to walk with assurance, even in the silence. Why? Because it trusts in God's perfect wisdom to govern what is hidden as well as what is revealed.

This kind of trust releases peace. We stop demanding constant confirmation. We stop measuring God's faithfulness by what we can feel or prove. Instead, we begin to say:

- "Father, I believe You are working even when I cannot trace it."

- "Your wisdom is enough to orchestrate what I cannot manage."

- "Your Hosts are active, even when I am unaware."

This is not passive ignorance. It is intentional dependence. Trusting in God's wisdom for the unseen does not mean withdrawing from action, it means acting in alignment with the conviction that God is always ahead of us, always surrounding us, always guiding us, whether we see it or not.

Practice trusting in the unseen by declaring: "God, I trust Your hand even when I cannot see Your movement, You are at work behind every veil."

The Gate of Number

4. Walking in Humility Like the Angels

The Hosts lead by bowing. Power wears humility in Heaven.

Angels model humility with majestic clarity. Though they excel in strength, wisdom, and splendor, they serve without pride. They obey without hesitation. They glorify God without drawing attention to themselves. Their greatness is not in their self-assertion, but in their total alignment with Heaven's will.

This is not accidental, it is their posture. Angels walk in what we could call perfect humility, not because they are ignorant or weak, but because they live in unbroken awareness of God's holiness. Every moment they spend in His presence deepens their reverence. Every mission they carry out reminds them of His glory. And they rejoice, not in their role, but in His rule.

We are invited to learn from this example.

Though we are not angels, we are called to walk in the same spirit of humility they embody. Like them, we are created to serve, to obey, to worship, and to move at the direction of the Lord. And like them, we will grow in spiritual authority as we remain low before the throne.

To walk in humility like the Angels is to:

Humility: The Call of the Incomprehensible

- Yield quickly when God speaks.

- Serve joyfully, even when unseen.

- Carry power without ego.

- Live in reverence without fear.

This posture is not only pleasing to God, it also positions us for alignment with the Hosts. Angels recognize in us what they themselves carry: the fragrance of humility. When we mirror their posture, we open the door to deeper partnership with them in the fulfillment of God's purposes.

Practice humility like the Angels today by asking God, "Help me to serve without needing attention, and to obey without hesitation, just like the Hosts who stand before You."

5. Cultivating Humility by Recognizing Our Role in God's Plan

Humility is not self-erasure, it is right-sized identity. One of the most powerful ways to cultivate humility is by recognizing that you are part of something vast and sacred: the unfolding plan of God. You matter. But you

Humility doesn't shrink you—it places you.

are not the center. That tension, of being deeply valued yet not ultimate, is the soil in which humility grows.

This realization can be both sobering and liberating.

God's plan spans generations, nations, spiritual dimensions, and eternal purposes. Yet within that majestic scope, He has given you a role. He has assigned you time, place, gifts, and relationships, all designed to fulfill your part in His redemptive mission. When we understand this, humility no longer feels like diminishment. It becomes joyful alignment.

You don't have to carry the whole story. You just have to play your part well.

This perspective removes pride, because the plan is not about us. But it also removes insecurity, because the plan includes us. And in this tension, we are trained to walk like Jesus, faithful, focused, and free from comparison.

Understanding your place also deepens your awareness of the broader team, including the Angelic Host. Angels know their place. They don't overstep, but neither do they underperform. They function in full confidence, under full submission. When we embrace our own assignment with similar reverence, we become trustworthy partners in the work of God.

Practice this today by praying: "Father, thank You for giving me a role in Your plan, help me to play it with faithfulness, not comparison, and with joy, not pride."

6. Inviting Angelic Cooperation in Our Mission

Humility does not exclude us from spiritual partnership, it prepares us for it. When we understand our role in God's plan, we can also begin to recognize and welcome the roles of others, including the Angelic Host. Angels have been assigned by God to serve His people, protect His purposes, and collaborate with those carrying out the Great Commission (Hebrews 1:14).

But cooperation with the Angelic Host is not automatic. It flows from revelation, alignment, and faith. As with any divine partnership, it begins with invitation.

We don't control the Angels- we align with their movement.

This invitation is not about control. It's about posture. We are not commanding Angels, we are agreeing with God's design. We are asking the Lord of Hosts to release His messengers into the assignments He has already prepared. When we walk in humility, we recognize that we need help, and we receive it without fear or pride.

The Gate of Number

Scripture gives us multiple examples of Angelic cooperation with human mission. From Daniel's intercession to Peter's deliverance, from Paul's guidance to John's visions, we see that Angels are often active where humility, faith, and obedience meet. That same pattern applies to us.

We invite Angelic cooperation when we:

- Ask God to release His Hosts in alignment with His will.

- Pray from a posture of reverence, not entitlement.

- Align our lives with Heaven's purposes, making room for Heaven's messengers.

This practice trains us to walk with spiritual awareness, not just of our personal devotion, but of God's broader operation. The humble heart says, "Lord, I'm ready. Use me. Surround me. Strengthen me through Your Word, Your Spirit, and Your Hosts."

Practice inviting this cooperation today by praying: "Father, I invite the help You've assigned, let Your Angels move with me as I walk in Your will."

Humility: The Call of the Incomprehensible

7. Believing in Angelic Protection in Spiritual Warfare

Humility is never passive; it prepares us for battle. While the proud assume they can fight alone, the humble acknowledge their need for God's covering, strength, and strategy. One of the most important ways this is expressed is through our faith in God's Angelic protection during spiritual warfare.

Scripture makes it clear: we are in a battle not against flesh and blood, but against spiritual forces of darkness (Ephesians 6:12). This is not metaphor, it is reality. Yet we are not defenseless. God has not only given us His Spirit and His Word; He has also appointed His Angels to guard, defend, and intervene.

To believe in Angelic protection is not to imagine fantasy, it is to trust the promises of God. Psalm 91:11 affirms this boldly: *"For He will command His angels concerning you to guard you in all your ways."* Humility receives this promise not as superstition, but as spiritual provision.

> **Believing in protection isn't superstition-it's Scripture.**

The humble don't fear mystery-they lean into it with trust.

In moments of conflict, pressure, or darkness, humble believers remember that they are not alone. They do not panic. They do not strive in fear. They stand in truth and call upon the covering of God.

This means praying boldly:

- "Lord of Hosts, surround me."

- "Let Your Angels war where I cannot."

- "Let every force of darkness be pushed back by the strength of Heaven's army."

This is not arrogance, it is alignment. The humble do not pretend to be strong on their own. But they believe deeply in the One who fights for them. And they trust that the Angelic Host is part of that holy warfare.

Practice this truth today by declaring: "God, I receive Your Angelic covering in every battle, thank You that I never stand alone."

The story of the Pale Blue Dot

There are moments in human history when science, wonder, and humility converge, when a simple image becomes a sacred mirror. One such moment happened in 1990, when the Voyager 1 spacecraft, nearing the edge of our solar system, turned its camera back toward Earth for one final photograph. The image it captured would become known as the "Pale Blue Dot."

Against the vast backdrop of space, Earth appears as nothing more than a tiny speck, a faint blue dot suspended in a beam of sunlight, barely visible among the stars. That single pixel contains all of human history: every nation and generation, every joy and every sorrow. All of it, reduced to a dot.

The image stunned the world. Not because it told us something new, but because it forced us to see what we already knew with greater clarity: we are small.

To some, that realization feels terrifying. How could something so small matter? But to those with eyes of faith, this perspective does not diminish significance, it reframes it. We are small, yes, but deeply loved by an infinite God. We are finite, yes, but included in an eternal plan. We are specks in the universe, but known by name, accompanied by Angels, and invited into partnership with the King of all creation.

The Pale Blue Dot reminds us that the Kingdom of God does not operate by human scale. Greatness, in Heaven's eyes, is not about size, power, or noise, it is about obedience, reverence, and humility. And while the world teaches us to

The Gate of Number

assert ourselves, the Gospel calls us to bow low, and there, find our truest identity.

As we consider the magnitude of the cosmos and the complexity of the Heavenly Host, we may feel like dots ourselves, overwhelmed, unseen, or too small to matter. But the God who flung the stars into space is the same God who calls us by name. He has assigned His Angels to walk with us. He has sent His Spirit to dwell within us. And He has wrapped us in a love that no scale can measure.

The question is not whether we are great enough. The question is whether we will trust the One who is. That trust, that humility, is the key that opens the door to collaboration with Heaven.

> ***"When I consider your heavens, the work of your fingers, the moon and the stars, which you have set in place, what is mankind that you are mindful of them, human beings that you care for them?"***
>
> ***(Psalm 8:3–4)***

And yet, He is mindful. And more than that, He invites us to walk with Him, not because we are great, but because He is.

An authority in Heaven and Earth

Humility does not cancel authority, it clarifies it. In the Kingdom of God, true authority is not based on personal greatness but on divine assignment. We do not operate in strength because of who we are in ourselves, but because of **who we are in Christ,** and the position He has given us within His sovereign plan.

Jesus, after His resurrection, declared:

> *"All authority in Heaven and on earth has been given to me. Therefore go..."*
>
> *(Matthew 28:18–19)*

This statement frames our commission. Our mission to disciple nations and fulfill God's purpose is anchored in **Christ's complete authority**, not just on earth, but in Heaven as well. This includes dominion over all created beings, visible and invisible, including the Angelic Host.

When we live in humility, we are not shrinking back from this reality, we are walking in it with reverent boldness. We do not command Angels in our own name, nor do we dismiss them as irrelevant. Instead, we align ourselves under the authority of Jesus, knowing that the same Jesus who sent us into the world is also the One to whom all the Angels bow.

The implication is profound: the authority of the Great Commission flows from a realm larger than we see, and its fulfillment depends on collaboration between Heaven and earth. The Hosts of Heaven are not distant spectators. They are part of the mission. And as we remain under Christ's authority, we will walk in increasing harmony with them, by His Word, by His Spirit, and for His glory.

Humility teaches us to lead as Jesus did, not by domination, but by submission. Jesus submitted to the Father perfectly, and in doing so, exercised perfect authority. Likewise, we grow in spiritual authority not by asserting ourselves, but by bowing lower, under His rule, under His timing, and within His design.

Our place in this heavenly order is not earned, it is given. And our confidence flows not from pride, but from the assurance that we have been sent, covered, and supported by the One who reigns over both the visible and the invisible realms.

Ready for Heavenly Partnership

Everything we've explored in this chapter, humility before mystery, trust in the unseen, sensitivity to God's order, and alignment with Heaven's movement, has been preparing us for this: partnership with the Angelic Host.

Heaven is not a spectator to what is happening on earth. Nor are we meant to walk out our callings disconnected from Heaven's help. We were never meant to bear the weight of the Great Commission alone. God's plan has always included divine-human cooperation. That includes His Spirit within us and His Angels around us.

But this partnership is not automatic. It flows from posture.

- Are we humble enough to follow when we don't fully understand?

- Are we spiritually alert enough to recognize Heaven's movement?

- Are we aligned enough with God's purposes to walk in harmony with His messengers?

The Heavenly Hosts are not interested in prideful ambition or theological debate. They move with clarity, purity, and obedience to God's voice. When they find that same posture in us, when we walk in humility, faith, reverence, and surrender, they come alongside us with joy. They strengthen, guard, guide, and fight, not because we deserve it, but because we are aligned with Heaven's mission.

Humility positions us to receive. And reception leads to cooperation.

If you want to walk with the Angelic Host, you must first walk humbly with your God (Micah 6:8). That is the starting point. And from there, every act of obedience, every prayer of trust, every step of surrender creates a bridge between the visible and the invisible, between your hands and Heaven's army.

You are not too small. You are not too weak.

You are being invited into something vast, eternal, and holy.

And if your heart says yes, the Hosts are already near.

THE POSTURE THAT UNLOCKS THE UNSEEN

Humility is more than a virtue, it is a gateway. It opens the heart to mystery, aligns the soul with Heaven, and prepares the Church for supernatural partnership.

> *Humility isn't just a virtue. It's the gate where Heaven meets earth.*

This chapter has led us along the path of this holy posture, revealing how humility invites us to:

- Respond rightly to complexity, not with fear or pride, but with trust and reverence.

- Embrace spiritual attitudes such as open-mindedness, curiosity, and resilience.

- Yield to God's wisdom even when we do not understand.

Humility: The Call of the Incomprehensible

- Recognize our role in God's larger plan, neither inflating nor minimizing ourselves.

- Walk like the Angels: faithful, obedient, surrendered.

- Invite and welcome the support of the Angelic Host in mission and warfare.

- Stand in authority under the rule of Christ, confident in both our calling and our covering.

We are not called to understand everything. But we are called to walk in alignment with the One who does. And that alignment requires humility, a posture low enough to hear God clearly, steady enough to trust Him deeply, and brave enough to step into partnership with the unseen.

> **Understanding isn't the calling-alignment is.**

The Angels are not looking for heroes. They are looking for disciples who walk as Jesus walked, meek, faithful, bold, and utterly surrendered to the Father's will. In that posture, Heaven draws near. The Kingdom advances. The Great Commission moves forward, not only by human effort, but by divine coordination.

So as you go from this chapter, go with a new posture: not of pride, not of striving, but of humble confidence.

The Gate of Number

Bow low

Stand firm.

Walk aligned.

And when you do, you will not walk alone. You will walk with the Host of Heaven.

> *"God opposes the proud but shows favor to the humble." (James 4:6)*

Let His favor rest upon you. Let His messengers walk beside you. And let His purpose be fulfilled through you, for the glory of the One who rules in Heaven and on earth.

Chapter 8
To Meditate Further

What would it look like for me to surrender my need for control in order to walk in step with the unseen?

How does embracing mystery strengthen my relationship with God and readiness to collaborate with Heaven?

Where have I resisted divine help because it came in ways I didn't expect or couldn't explain?

How can humility reshape the way I approach leadership, intercession, and mission?

What daily habit can I cultivate to remain grounded in humility even while walking in divine authority?

(Isaiah 55:8–9, Matthew 11:29, Proverbs 3:5–6, Romans 11:33, 2 Kings 5:10–14, Philippians 2:3–4, Micah 6:8)

Conclusion To The First Gate: The Gate of Number

There is an intrinsic value in seeking from the Lord an understanding of the Heavenly Hosts. However, the quest of this series did not start with the urge to know more about them but instead with the one of knowing how to fulfill the creator's purpose and the Lord's command for His disciples. It appears that none may be completed without an adequate coming into terms with who they are not only by themselves but moreover in relation to man. The answers can be found through a variety of many ways and places. It would be found preferably in Scriptures and in God's movements in Creation. The answers take a special importance and meaning from the lips of the Master, the maker of the command. This book sought-after the intentions behind those words and the unarticulated nuances behind them. This book started the series by giving attention to a specific grammatical device used exclusively by the Master in reference to the Heavenly Hosts: the plural. The insights gained offers the possibility to construct paths that connect dimensions of the existences in which God's intention had always been to be the experience of man at creation. Yet, while the possibilities are graciously offered by

> *The mission begins with obedience, but it advances with Angels.*

the One who moves the Angels and tells everything to His investigative disciples (John 16:13), we need humility and the desire to look where God leads, even when everything else points somewhere else that we expect. What the Heavens hold is not necessarily hidden but is not necessarily given and may be nothing of what we expect. Such is the image of the gates of Jesus references to Angels in the New Testament among which is the His language use that we explored with the guidance of the Holy Spirit. This exploration unveils some needed breakthroughs into the possibilities left for disciples to collaborate for and more effectively with the invisible co-servants with whom he is called to fulfill God's program in creation.

Four postures open Heaven's gate: reverence, unity, assurance, and humility.

The connection with the heavenly helpers requires the understanding of the value systems and descriptive realities of their existences and operations. Such an understanding causes the taking of the right posture, the positioning into the right place where doors open to connect with reality. The connection with Heavenly Hosts starts with the establishing of the proper inner and outer environment of such a connection. The inner environment, which we just mentioned earlier, needs to become manifested in life direction, choices, behavior and even its lifestyle. Jesus's words intended to teach the believers just that.

The Gate of Number

The gate cracked open by this book shows some pillars of the values system of the Heavenly Hosts: Reverence, Unity (Of purpose), Faith (Assurance in God's capacity) and Humility.

The posture of God towards His creation and the model of Jesus are the prime example of this character.

> *The multitude is not infinite, but it is always enough.*

Jesus revealed it through the examples of His words and life to show believers a path to follow to identify with the heavenlies attitudes. In men, it blends honor, gratitude, awe and commitment towards the Creation (including the God, the Hosts of Heavens, other men and nature), as appropriate to each or towards a cause.

> *Humility is the lens that lets us see Heaven's complex design.*

Unity is the characteristic feature of Heavens. It starts in the examples of the trinity and extends to the nature of order in the heavenly realms. The existence of the Heavenly Hosts is intertwined in a single existential identity. The body of their creation, incredible in beauty and power, exists as such because it is headed by one single purpose: fulfilling God's will to the end. This feature has appeared to be the desire of God for the body of believers who belong to it whether they are aware or not. Thus, being aware of it is a crucial factor in the creation of

Conclusion to The First Gate

the right attitude, purpose, and assurance in fulfilling heaven lifestyle proper for service and collaboration with the hosts of God.

There is no greater assurance that can be provided than the one that is revealed through the multitude as expressed throughout the Scriptures. The extra-sensorial reality of Heavens makes it difficult to understand the nature of quantity in such dimensions. The number gates also display the image of the multitude which is found in divine display of capacity and assurance. The numbers are not infinite, yet they are not closed. The reality is that there is enough for every single cosmic need, those that we know and those still unknown. The thrust into obedience to God's will is the key to generate the needed servant or to activate it and see it manifest. The pillar of sufficiency shows that there will always be more than enough in terms of help when believers are geared toward the accomplishment of God's Commission.

> *Heaven's virtues are resisted because they unlock divine partnership.*

While these features may be appealing and appalling in terms of their potency, they are only a limited portion of the divine wisdom hidden in the nature of the things in Heaven which God wants to see represented on earth. The pillar of humility is the posture in fact of the revelation about the multiplex realities behind the singularity of the existence of

> *The way we use words can open gates-or close them.*

the Heavenly Hosts. The posture of humility that it calls to is also a characteristic trait that is required to create the right environment for identification of the heavenly and earthly family of God in its fulfillment of its calling and destiny. Without such humility even the posture that sees is impossible and receiving the faith to manifest a fruitful and effective relation with those who are called to be our co-laborers, brothers, and servants is stranded.

At times such as the ones experienced in these generations, these pillars are a prophetic call. God does not back up on His calling and graces and His plans to unite His divine family in heaven and earth. This is a generation where more than ever such communication and connection is necessary. It holds the keys to overcome the ardor of the adversary. There is no confusion over while such heavenly virtues, behaviors and focuses are so much battled down. They hide the mystery that unlocks our heavenly capacities. May these revelations be a tool to construct them where they lack and instill them in the generation for its future.

Many disciples understood just that. The apostles who wrote about Jeus words left hints, lessons, and revelations about this. Diving specifically into this has been articulated through history for the disciple's transformation and connection. Some of the revelations of this book resonated

Conclusion to The First Gate

with ideas and guidance I had heard before in one way or another and others were new to my spirit.

The Number Gate is another demonstration of the power of the choice of language. The insight gained

> *Speaking with reverence invites Heaven's help.*

through these words teaches wisdom and discernment, recognizing the significance of words and their impact on opening revelations and unlocking or blocking destinies. The stylistic choices that revealed these lessons serve as a reminder to choose our words carefully and to use language that uplifts and honors God's creation. Whether we use those words to speak about another person, physical or spiritual entities, to make a motivational speech or to make a vow, the words chosen may be the key to Heaven and moreover to our destiny. Without doubt, as His followers, we are called to emulate His example and strive to embody these qualities in our own lives, honoring and respecting all aspects of God's magnificent creation. Divine help and provision is available because it is crucial to the full picture of God's destiny for us

EPILOGUE

As I close on this volume, I would like to linger a bit more on Carl Sagan, the author of "Pale Blue Dot: A Vision of the Human Future in Space"[9]. He was brought up in a family that was identified as liberal Jews in their religious affiliation. His own religious stand stayed ambiguous all his life. In his book on the picture taken by Voyager 1, he wrote: "We are a way for the cosmos to know itself." He made a statement which scope, maybe, unknowingly, resonates beyond the dimensions of both our existence and creation. The man became also associated with the expression: "billions and billions" a derivative of his original "billions upon billions" a number that is sourced in his contemplation of the celestial lights and that reveal the intriguing reality of numbers associated with them. He also wrote: "Plainly, the world held wonders of a kind I had never guessed. How could a tone become a picture and light become a noise?" This is true not only of the material world but also of the heavenly one and the connection between them. As brethren of Angels and heirs in their capacities as the Malaks of old and as Holy Ones bestowed with the capacities of the Holy Spirit let's grown in the fellowship of this family, hear visions, see God voice and complete the task at hand with Heavenly capacities. Let us continue our journey of discovery, in humility letting the tribute to numbers open the gate for the promised of God who reveals:

"The secret things belong unto the LORD our God: but those things which are revealed belong unto us and to our children forever, that we may do all the words of this law." (Deuteronomy 29:29 KJV)

APPENDIX

Glossary of Key Terms

Abraham

The patriarch of Israel, father of faith, whose trust in God's promises foreshadows salvation by faith in Christ.

Pages: 51

Adonai

Hebrew for 'Lord' or 'Master,' emphasizing God's authority; in the book, it highlights reverence and submission.

Pages: 58, 62, 67

Alignment

Harmony with God's will that attracts Angelic presence and brings clarity and authority.

Pages: 9, 24, 33, 34, 41, 71, 78, 88, 92, 93, 95, 97, 128, 134, 149, 152, 157, 160, 161, 170, 173, 178, 186, 187, 191, 194, 195, 199, 203, 224, 225, 230, 232, 235, 238, 242, 244, 245, 248, 253, 255, 269, 279, 286

Almighty

Title meaning 'All-Sufficient One' or 'Ruler of All'; assures believers of God's supreme power behind Angelic collaboration.

Pages: 212, 275

Angels

Heaven's emissaries, referenced in the plural, signifying collective collaboration and order in Heaven's mission.

Pages: 11, 15, 16, 18, 19, 20, 25, 26, 29, 30, 31, 33, 34, 35, 37, 38, 39, 40, 42, 44, 46, 48, 49, 50, 51, 52, 53, 57, 58, 59, 60, 61, 63, 64, 66, 67, 68, 69, 70, 71, 72, 74, 75, 76, 77, 78, 83, 84, 85, 87, 88, 89, 90, 91, 92, 93, 95, 96, 97, 102, 105, 106, 108, 111, 112, 113, 117, 120, 121, 127, 129, 130, 131, 133, 134, 136, 140, 142, 145, 146, 148, 149, 153, 154, 155, 156, 157, 158, 160, 162, 163, 166, 168, 170, 171, 172, 174, 178, 183, 184, 186, 187, 190, 191, 192, 194, 195, 201, 202, 203, 204, 205, 209, 210, 211, 215, 218, 220, 222, 224, 225, 226, 227, 228, 229, 230, 233, 234, 236, 237, 238, 240, 241, 242, 243, 244, 246, 249, 250, 251, 252, 253, 255, 256, 257, 258, 260, 261, 269, 279, 283, 284

Assurance

Trusting God's promises; believers gain confidence by recognizing the vast Host with them.

Pages: 25, 27, 41, 103, 110, 111, 112, 114, 116, 118, 119, 121, 208, 209, 210, 212, 213, 214, 215, 216, 217, 218, 220, 222, 223, 224, 226, 227, 228, 229, 230, 232, 234, 236, 238, 240, 242, 243, 244, 245, 246, 248, 250, 252, 254, 256, 257, 258, 260

Carl Sagan

Astronomer cited for awe at cosmic scale, paralleling biblical revelation of innumerable Angels.

Epilogue

Cherubim

Angelic beings guarding sacred spaces, linked to God's throne, plural form enhances majesty.

Pages: 48, 64, 67, 130, 131

Christ

The Anointed One (Messiah), central figure who commands the Hosts and directs divine mission.

Pages: 9, 10, 17, 20, 21, 29, 33, 35, 49, 66, 74, 95, 98, 109, 112, 117, 119, 120, 131, 133, 134, 136, 158, 170, 186, 189, 191, 204, 225, 274, 276

Collaboration

Partnership between humanity and Angels; essential for fulfilling the Great Commission.

Pages: 9, 18, 19, 27, 29, 34, 37, 38, 39, 42, 49, 53, 71, 78, 91, 95, 98, 146, 152, 158, 159, 160, 162, 167, 183, 184, 185, 186, 202, 226, 227, 236, 239, 265, 266, 267, 270, 271, 278

Complexity

A divine principle seen in creation and Angelic orders, revealing God's infinite wisdom.

Pages: 25, 33, 41, 53, 126, 127, 128, 129, 131, 134, 135, 136, 137, 141, 142, 143, 144, 145, 146, 148, 153, 267, 268, 270, 271

Daniel

Prophet and author of the Old Testament book, model of devotion and revealer of God's sovereignty.

Pages: 111, 119, 211, 229, 230, 234, 242, 252, 256

Dimension

Describes layered realities of Heaven and Earth, showing that Angelic operations connect realms.

Pages: 24, 33, 34, 41, 53, 102, 130, 131, 135, 213, 223, 224, 230, 277

Divine Family

God's household, including Himself, His Son, the Spirit, Angels, and redeemed humanity.

Pages: 35

Dominions

One Angelic order in the nine choirs, symbolizing delegated authority in Heaven's structure.

Pages: 130, 131

Elohim

Plural form of 'El,' conveying majesty; in the book, key to divine collaboration and plurality.

Pages: 58, 62, 65, 67, 73

Ephesians

Paul's letter emphasizing identity in Christ, unity of the Church, and the armor of God.

Pages: 130, 133, 135, 136, 171, 225

Evangelism

Proclaiming the Gospel; supported by Angels in the book as part of Heaven's mission.

Pages: 219, 232, 233, 261

Faith

Confidence in God's promises; a channel for assurance and Angelic collaboration.

Pages: 9, 17, 25, 27, 29, 49, 70, 77, 104, 109, 112, 114, 115, 116, 118, 119, 122, 131, 137, 139, 140, 142, 144, 146, 148, 149, 152, 157, 185, 197, 199, 201, 202, 203, 210, 215, 219, 221, 223, 224, 225, 226, 227, 230, 231, 232, 233, 234, 235, 237, 238, 239, 241, 245, 248, 249, 250, 252, 253, 254, 257, 259, 261, 267, 275, 277, 281, 285, 286

Fellowship

Communion in Christ that extends to participation with the Host of Heaven.

Pages: 10, 20, 172, 177, 270, 280, 281, 282

Genesis

The first book of the Bible, laying the foundation for covenant and God's purposes.

Pages: 51, 62, 130, 157, 204

Glory

The radiant expression of God's nature; reflected in the majesty of His Host.

Pages: 24, 54, 57, 59, 60, 62, 63, 64, 67, 68, 70, 74, 87, 89, 92, 94, 95, 97, 98, 102, 103, 117, 131, 143, 145, 153, 162, 166, 174, 204, 212, 216, 234

Heavenly Host

The innumerable yet ordered company of Angels, active in God's purposes on Earth.

Pages: 9, 15, 25, 32, 35, 52, 64, 68, 72, 77, 84, 93, 97, 106, 112, 135, 141, 143, 152, 153, 154, 159, 160, 162, 166, 187, 188, 190, 194, 210, 211, 223, 226, 243, 274, 275, 279

Holy Ones

A reverent title for Angels and God, emphasizing nearness to holiness.

Pages: 63, 133

Isaiah

Prophetic book emphasizing holiness, judgment, and messianic hope fulfilled in Christ.

Pages: 52, 63, 108, 130, 169, 233, 269, 270, 273, 275

Jesus

Son of God, Savior of the world, whose life, death, and resurrection bring salvation.

Pages: 15, 18, 24, 25, 26, 29, 31, 32, 33, 34, 35, 37, 38, 39, 40, 44, 46, 47, 48, 49, 50, 51, 52, 54, 57, 58, 59, 60, 61, 64, 66, 67, 68, 69, 70, 71, 72, 74, 75, 76, 77, 78, 82, 83, 84, 85, 86, 87, 88, 89, 90, 91, 92, 93, 97, 98, 102, 109, 110, 118, 138, 140, 145, 153, 154, 155, 160, 162, 163, 166, 167, 168, 170, 172, 183, 185, 186, 187, 204, 218, 223, 224, 235, 247, 284

John

Apostle, author of the Gospel, epistles, and Revelation, emphasizing truth and love.

Pages: 50, 68, 109, 110, 111, 112, 117, 118, 119, 133, 155, 172, 185, 197, 201

Kingdom

God's reign and rule; relational and collaborative between Heaven and Earth.

Pages: 9, 21, 24, 40, 49, 88, 91, 93, 96, 97, 127, 128, 134, 147, 153, 178, 179, 184, 187, 199, 202, 212, 215, 223, 225, 226, 230, 244, 251, 266, 280, 282

Lamb

Title for Christ, fulfilled in His sacrifice, magnified in Angelic worship.

Pages: 112, 117

Legions of Angels

Term used by Jesus, expressing immense Angelic support available to Him.

Pages: 87, 90, 155, 218

Lord of Hosts

Title portraying God as commander of Heaven's armies.

Pages: 63, 212, 232, 233, 241, 244, 249, 252, 254, 257

Louis Berkhof

Reformed theologian, cited for his affirmation of Angelology in evangelical tradition.

Pages: 30

Mark

The second Gospel, fast-paced, portraying Jesus as the Servant of God.

Pages: 20, 50, 87, 89, 134, 135, 144, 170, 177, 187, 270, 271, 282

Mary

Mother of Jesus, model of obedience and faith, chosen to bear the Messiah.

Pages: 75, 173, 185

Messengers

Angelic designation from Hebrew 'malak,' meaning messenger.

Pages: 38, 39, 77, 95, 127, 134, 135, 171, 187, 193, 224, 254, 286

Michael Heiser

Biblical scholar cited for his work on divine council and Angelology.

Pages: 132

Ministering Spirits

Description of Angels as sent to serve those inheriting salvation.

Pages: 34, 158, 236, 237, 241, 249, 261

Multiplexity

Heaven's richness and multidimensional nature, calling for humility.

Pages: 25, 126, 127, 128, 129, 135, 140, 147, 150, 275

New International Version

Modern translation balancing readability and accuracy; default in the book.

Number

Theological category conveying God's order, majesty, and assurance through numbers.

Pages: 7, 8, 9, 11, 13, 14, 15, 17, 19, 21, 23, 24, 25, 27, 29, 31, 33, 35, 37, 38, 39, 40, 41, 42, 44, 45, 46, 47, 48, 49, 50, 51, 52, 53, 54, 57, 59, 60, 61, 62, 63, 64, 65, 67, 69, 71, 73, 75, 77, 79, 81, 83, 85, 86, 87, 89, 91, 93, 95, 97, 99, 102, 103, 104, 105, 106, 107, 108, 109, 110, 111, 112, 113, 114, 115, 116, 117, 118, 119, 120, 121, 122, 123, 127, 129, 131, 133, 135, 137, 139, 141, 143, 145, 147, 149, 152, 153, 154, 155, 156, 157, 158, 159, 160, 161, 162, 163, 165, 166, 167, 169, 171, 173, 175, 177, 179, 183, 185, 187, 189, 190, 191, 193, 195, 197, 199, 201, 203, 205, 209, 211, 213, 214, 215, 217, 219, 220, 221, 222, 223, 225, 227, 229, 231, 233, 235, 237, 239, 241, 242, 243, 245, 247, 249, 250, 251, 253, 255, 257, 258, 259, 261, 263, 265, 267, 269, 271, 273, 275, 277, 279, 281, 283, 285

Obedience

Willing submission to God's will, modeled by Angels, essential for collaboration.

Pages: 41, 71, 95, 127, 192, 193, 197, 199, 201, 210, 220, 224, 225, 226, 235, 247, 253, 265, 266, 285

Peter

Apostle and leader of the early Church, restored after denial of Christ.

Pages: 74, 202

Pluralis Excellentiae

The 'majestic plural,' highlighting divine greatness and multiplicity.

Pages: 51, 53, 57, 60, 61, 63, 64, 65, 66, 83

Powers

An Angelic designation from the nine choirs, pointing to authority roles.

Pages: 110, 130, 131, 136, 225, 237

Principalities

Angelic designation symbolizing delegated authority within Heaven's structure.

Pages: 130, 131, 225

Pseudo-Dionysius

Christian mystic whose writings shaped Angelological tradition.

Pages: 130

Purpose

God's intention for His people and creation, requiring Angelic partnership.

Pages: 31, 32, 39, 40, 42, 47, 48, 53, 71, 82, 83, 85, 88, 90, 91, 94, 102, 103, 108, 111, 113, 114, 118, 120, 122, 128, 131, 133, 135, 137, 141, 142, 143, 145, 147, 153, 161, 167, 173, 179, 183, 184, 186, 187, 190, 195, 196, 202, 209, 211, 212, 215, 216, 217, 218, 221, 222, 223, 224, 226, 230, 235, 241, 250, 251, 254, 260, 277, 282, 284

Revelation

Final book of the Bible, depicting Christ's victory and new creation.

Pages: *19, 20, 27, 37, 40, 41, 45, 46, 51, 52, 53, 59, 61, 69, 72, 73, 76, 83, 85, 92, 97, 102, 106, 107, 108, 109, 110, 112, 113, 116, 117, 118, 119, 120, 121, 126, 129, 130, 139, 140, 141, 144, 148, 149, 153, 154, 157, 161, 167, 204, 211, 222, 224, 226, 230, 232, 234, 236, 238, 242, 243, 252, 254, 256, 260, 271, 274, 276, 277, 279, 286*

Reverence

Atmosphere of holiness that draws Angels and aligns believers with Heaven.

Pages: *24, 26, 29, 31, 40, 41, 42, 44, 53, 57, 59, 61, 63, 64, 65, 66, 67, 68, 69, 70, 71, 72, 74, 75, 76, 77, 78, 86, 91, 92, 93, 97, 98, 102, 107, 131, 132, 137, 141, 143, 148, 153, 166, 167, 168, 169, 170, 171, 172, 173, 174, 175, 176, 177, 178, 179, 180, 190, 194, 197, 199, 201, 202, 203, 240, 259, 265, 268, 273, 275, 276, 278, 279*

Romans

Paul's letter emphasizing justification by faith and holy living.

Pages: *59, 133, 227, 272*

Son of the Living God

Title affirming Jesus' divine identity and authority over Angels.

Pages: *74*

Sons of God

Biblical title for celestial beings and believers, stressing unity in Christ.

Pages: 48, 133

Spirits

Title underscoring Angels' spiritual nature and ministering role.

Pages: 30, 34, 133, 158, 236, 237, 241, 242, 249, 261

Spiritual Warfare

Ongoing struggle where Angels aid the Church against evil powers.

Pages: 115, 210, 217, 220, 227, 229, 230, 231, 232, 261

Stars

Symbol of heavenly beings and divine design; God names and numbers them.

Pages: 8, 24, 51, 52, 104, 105, 120, 121, 133, 141

The First and the Last

Title of Christ, emphasizing His eternal sovereignty.

Pages: 110

The Living God

Title distinguishing the true God from idols, emphasizing vitality.

Pages: 74, 243, 257

The Living One

Title of Christ in Revelation, proclaiming victory over death.

The Scriptures 2009

Version restoring Hebrew names of God and Messiah; cited for depth.

Thrones

Angelic order symbolizing governance and authority in Heaven.

Pages: 130, 131, 231, 256

Trinity

God revealed as Father, Son, and Spirit, unity in multiplicity.

Pages: 24, 26, 88, 92, 93, 185, 186, 187

Virtues

Angelic designation in the nine choirs, reflecting Heaven's richness.

Pages: 130, 131, 192

Watchers

Scriptural Angelic title highlighting vigilance and identity.

Pages: 133

Winds

Angelic designation symbolizing mission and movement.

Pages: 9, 133

Worship

Reverent recognition of God's worth, joined by Angels in harmony.

Pages: 76, 84, 92, 112, 113, 116, 117, 119, 140, 170, 172, 174, 175, 177, 183, 194, 198, 201, 202, 203, 237, 239, 240, 242, 244, 245, 254, 255, 257, 265, 276, 279, 284

Community & Movement

This book is not the closing of a journey but the opening of one. The revelations of the Gate of Number are meant to awaken us, not to a solitary pursuit, but to a shared walk with the Heavenly Host and with one another. Every page points beyond itself-toward a living movement of collaboration that stretches from the individual believer to the global Body of Christ.

Winds International was birthed from this same conviction: that Heaven's purposes are realized when God's people move together in reverence, alignment, and mission. It is a space where disciples, leaders, and communities are equipped to discern the movements of Heaven and to join them on Earth. Through training, creative initiatives, and partnerships, Winds International seeks to nurture a generation ready to walk with Angels for the sake of God's Kingdom.

This book is also part of a larger unfolding vision-*The Four Gates to the Heavenlies* series. Each Gate reveals a dimension of Heaven's design, drawing the Church into deeper collaboration with the Hosts of God and into greater clarity about our shared mission. The Gate of Number is only the first step; what lies ahead is a path of discovery that widens into purpose, unity, and identity.

You are invited to take your place in this movement. Reading is only the beginning. The Hosts of Heaven are near, the Great Commission is before us, and the journey is ours to walk together.

EXPLORE THE JOURNEY FURTHER

The Gate of Number is only the beginning of a greater revelation. *The Four Gates to the Heavenlies* series is designed to guide you step by step into deeper understanding, alignment, and collaboration with the Heavenly Host. Each Gate opens a fresh dimension of God's design and equips you to walk it out in your daily life and mission.

- **The Gate of Number** – Discover how God communicates His majesty, order, and assurance through numbers and through the multitudes of His Angels.

- **The Gate of Reference** – Learn how God uses symbols, names, and divine references to connect Heaven's purposes with earthly realities.

- **The Gate of Function** – Explore the practical operations of the Heavenly Host and how their roles intersect with the mission of the Church.

- **The Gate of Identity** – Enter into the mystery of who we are in Christ and how our identity resonates with Heaven's family and destiny.

Together, these Gates form a pathway of revelation that invites the believer into maturity, unity, and active partnership with the Hosts of God for the fulfillment of the Great Commission.

In addition, the **official book website** provides extended resources to enrich your journey, including:

- Study guides and reflection questions for personal or group use.

- Articles and teaching videos expanding on key themes.

- Updates on training opportunities and Winds International initiatives.

- A community space to connect with others walking through the Four Gates.

Let each book and resource move you further into alignment with Heaven's purposes. This journey is not meant to be traveled alone-join a community of readers, intercessors, and leaders across the world who are responding to God's invitation to walk with Angels.

About the Author

Antonin K. Azoti is the Co-Founder and President of Winds International, a movement dedicated to equipping leaders, churches, and communities for transformation. A pastor, teacher, and trainer, he has ministered and taught across Africa, Europe, and North America, including years of service as an educator in the United States. He is also pursuing doctoral research at Leiden University, bringing together academic rigor, theological insight, and practical ministry experience. As the visionary behind *The Four Gates to the Heavenlies* series, Antonin carries a passion to awaken the Body of Christ to the reality of Heaven's partnership.

www.ingramcontent.com/pod-product-compliance
Lightning Source LLC
Chambersburg PA
CBHW031706230426
43668CB00006B/125